Racial Profiling

Issues in Crime & Justice

Series Editor
Gregg Barak, Eastern Michigan University

As we embark upon the twentieth-first century, the meanings of crime continue to evolve and our approaches to justice are in flux. The contributions to this series focus their attention on crime and justice as well as on crime control and prevention in the context of a dynamically changing legal order. Across the series, there are books that consider the full range of crime and criminality and that engage a diverse set of topics related to the formal and informal workings of the administration of criminal justice. In an age of globalization, crime and criminality are no longer confined, if they ever were, to the boundaries of single nation-states. As a consequence, while many books in the series will address crime and justice in the United States, the scope of these books will accommodate a global perspective and they will consider such eminently global issues such as slavery, terrorism, or punishment. Books in the series are written to be used as supplements in standard undergraduate and graduate courses in criminology and criminal justice and related courses in sociology. Some of the standard courses in these areas include: introduction to criminal justice, introduction to law enforcement, introduction to corrections, juvenile justice, crime and delinquency, criminal law, white collar, corporate, and organized crime.

TITLES IN SERIES:

Effigy, by Allison Cotton

Perverts and Predators, by Laura J. Zilney and Lisa Anne Zilney

The Prisoners' World, by William Tregea and Marjorie Larmour

Racial Profiling, by Karen S. Glover

Racial Profiling

Research, Racism, and Resistance

Karen S. Glover

ROWMAN & LITTLEFIELD PUBLISHERS, INC.
Lanham • Boulder • New York • Toronto • Plymouth, UK

ROWMAN & LITTLEFIELD PUBLISHERS, INC.

Published in the United States of America
by Rowman & Littlefield Publishers, Inc.
A wholly owned subsidiary of The Rowman & Littlefield Publishing Group, Inc.
4501 Forbes Boulevard, Suite 200, Lanham, Maryland 20706
www.rowmanlittlefield.com

Estover Road
Plymouth PL6 7PY
United Kingdom

British Library Cataloguing in Publication Information Available

Library of Congress Cataloging-in-Publication Data

Glover, Karen S., 1964–
Racial profiling : research, racism, and resistance / Karen S. Glover.
p. cm.
Includes bibliographical references and index.
ISBN 978-0-7425-6105-2 (cloth : alk. paper) — ISBN 978-0-7425-6106-9 (pbk. : alk. paper) — ISBN 978-0-7425-9964-2 (electronic)
1. Racial profiling in law enforcement. I. Title.
HV7936.R3G56 2009
363.2′3089—dc22 2009005676

Printed in the United States of America

∞™ The paper used in this publication meets the minimum requirements of American National Standard for Information Sciences—Permanence of Paper for Printed Library Materials, ANSI/NISO Z39.48-1992.

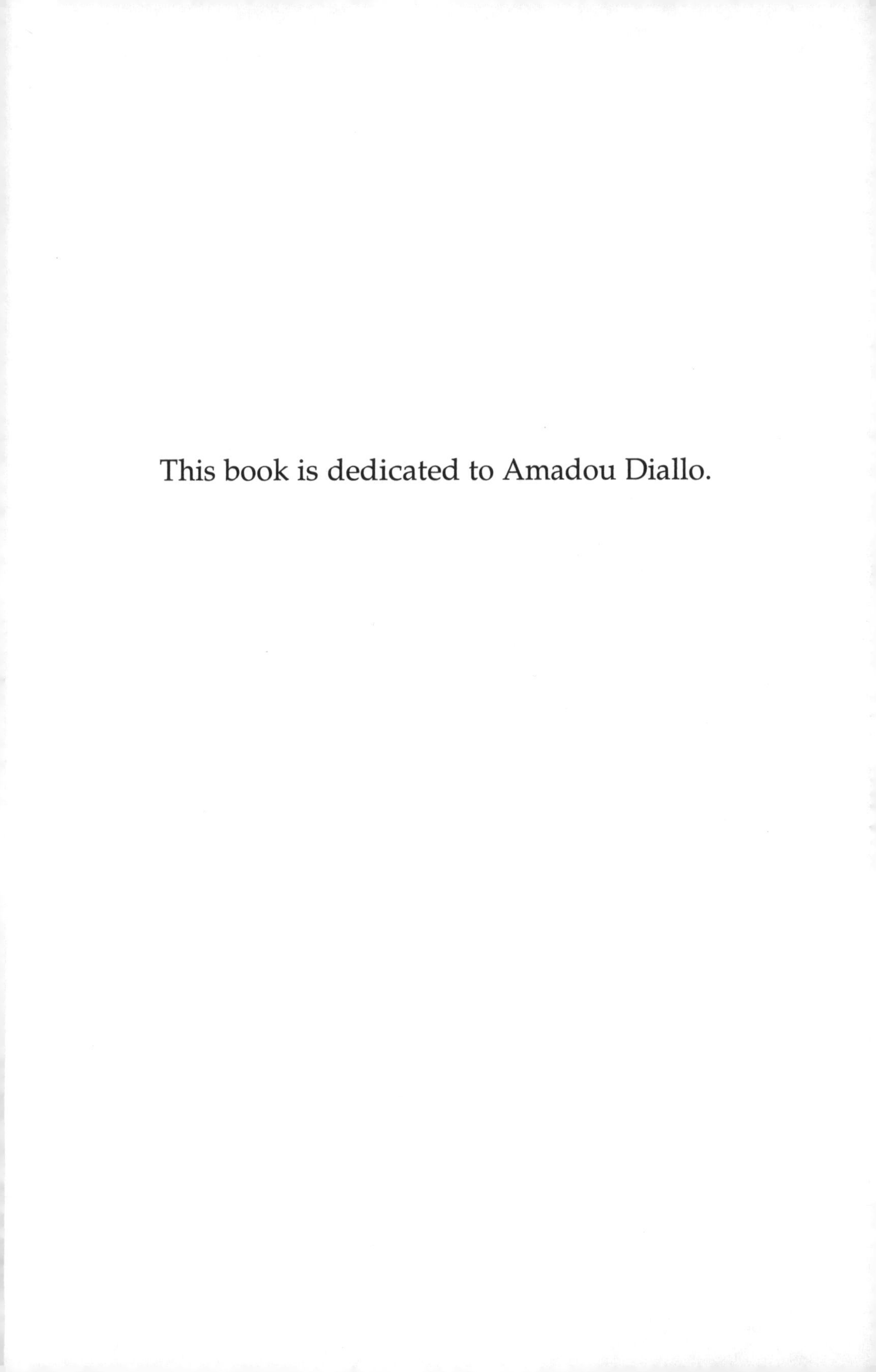

This book is dedicated to Amadou Diallo.

Contents

Acknowledgments

I am grateful to the following folks for supporting me along this particular path, including those who reviewed earlier incarnations of this work: Gregg Barak, Bilaye Benibo, Eduardo Bonilla-Silva, Kimberly Brown, Sharon Elise, David Geronimo Embrick, Joe Feagin, Mark Fossett, Holly Foster, Sarah Gatson, Marco Portales, Dudley Poston, Missy Rice, Katheryn Russell-Brown, Rogelio Saenz, and Sarah Stanton. To the folks I met in the field, thank you for trusting me with your thoughts—I hope I do your experiences justice. To all of my students, from the alternative schools, to the juvenile court, to the students at California State University, San Marcos, thank you for letting me be me with you and thank you for your teachings. I would also like to acknowledge my colleagues in the departments of Sociology at California State University, San Marcos, and Texas A&M University for your many realms of generosity and support. Finally, to my friends and family. I love all of you.

Introduction

To a Critical Race Criminology

I was outside the grand building that housed the Department of Sociology at Texas A&M University, a very white space indeed, going over comments from my advisor on my master's thesis. A black man, one of the few on campus and whom I, a white woman, had noticed on occasion, approached. We struck up a brief conversation and he asked what I was working on. I told him it was a study about racial profiling. "Oh, I have a lot of stories about that," he stated. "Really?" I asked, obviously signaling some genuine surprise to him. He looked at me intently then laughed—"Yes! I'm a black man!"

And there it was. The experiential, the narrative, my naiveté as a young scholar. . . . I recognized that even though I'd been pouring through the mainstream criminological literature on police–minority relations for quite some time at that point, I just didn't get it.

This book was provoked years ago after my attendance at an annual meeting of the American Society of Criminology.[1] At the meeting, I attended as many sessions on racial profiling—the hot agenda of the day—as I could fit in. I left that meeting and others like it very frustrated and angered at the lack of discussion of *race* in this collective scholarship concerning *race*.[2] The race-as-a-variable paradigm in criminology dominated.[3]

More recent inspiration is due to an edited volume of works by race scholars Tukufu Zuberi and Eduardo Bonilla-Silva entitled *White Logic, White Methods: Racism and Methodology*.[4] The thrust of *White Logic, White*

Methods, as well as earlier conceptualizations by Joe Feagin[5] about the *white racial frame* that orients American society, makes clear that our scientific knowledge of society, including our knowledge of the "making, breaking, and social reactions to law . . . ," is founded on white supremacy ideology. As with Katheryn Russell's[6] conceptualization of the *ethical imperative* that advocates for greater accountability in the sciences when racialized research masquerades as scientific fact, Zuberi and Bonilla-Silva make a call to critical scholars to uncover, illuminate, and contest this white logic orientation as a step toward a more just society. In attempting to heed that call specific to the research on racial profiling, I engage in the following in what might be considered *critical race criminology*.

Russell's call for a black criminology[7] serves as inspiration for what I am calling a *critical race criminology*. A critical race criminology, like the critical race studies it reflects, places race at the fore of social analyses. It is concerned with the representations of race, crime, law, and justice specifically as they operate in the production of knowledge. Critical race criminology specifically addresses traditional and contemporary examinations of race in criminology and contests the ways the discipline produces and represents race by focusing on and indeed validating experiential knowledge via the social narrative of marginalized communities. As such, this scholarship falls in line with other critical-oriented works that examine the various forms of oppression in the social arena by turning a critical eye to hegemonic discourses.[8] As a guide to the development of a critical race criminology, Russell's concept of *affirmative race law*[9] is useful. As a theoretical construct, affirmative race law involves two distinct dimensions: one concerned with critically analyzing phenomenon already in operation and one concerned with the development and employment of alternative practice to forward social justice. Specifically, the first dimension is to unveil the way law has traditionally been used in racialization and criminalization by the state. The other dimension involves the implementation of legislation that specifically counters racial discrimination, including these historical and contemporary patterns of legislation racism. Similarly, I formulate two distinct dimensions of a critical race criminology. The first is to reveal the traditional modes of representation that the disciplines of sociology, criminology, and law have developed on race, crime, and justice. The second component of a critical race criminology is to reveal, primarily through the narrative, the experiential—the everydayness—of racializing and criminalizing processes to further our collective understanding of racial profiling. Examples of work of the former that I consider as falling under the rubric of a critical race criminology include Jeannette Covington's *Racial Classification in Criminology: The Reproduction of Racialized Crime*[10] and, of the latter, Wendy Moore's recent *Reproducing Racism: White Space, Elite Law Schools, and Racial Inequality*.[11]

CRIMINOLOGY, RACE, AND SOCIAL REPRODUCTION

I contend that criminology as a discipline exists in a racial vacuum yet criminology is obsessed with race. This is particularly true of the current body of racial profiling studies that quickly ascended to a prominent position in the late twentieth- and early twenty-first-century American criminological agenda. Hypercognizant of race yet void of comprehensive analysis of the operation of race in the post-Civil Rights era, criminologists succeed at establishing, maintaining, and reinforcing associations between racial status and crime. With the exception of the critical lens engaged by the likes of W. E. B. DuBois and other scholars of color, *white* sociology is guided by the white racial frame that organizes whites' view of the world. As a subset of sociology, criminology has demonstrated a near obsession with the race–crime dyad from the earliest times to present day. Yet, there is little attention directed to understanding race in and of itself given its concentration in contemporary era perspectives on crime, both in academe and in the public domain. Hence the often-walked trail of race–crime scholarship in criminology leads us to a very limited picture of the complex operations that structure race and crime. It is imperative that mainstream criminology turns a lens on itself and acknowledges its own function in the reproduction of racial inequality. Failing to do so facilitates the current rise in criminal "justice" programs in academe, especially the social control-oriented *cop shops* that generate substantial sums for our university systems. This tendency equates to new generations of researchers and policy makers who accept the unexamined life of race and crime as it is currently presented in the criminology and criminal justice disciplines.[12] A critical race criminology, as forwarded here, is fundamentally about contextualizing law and crime concerns within a race-conscious framework.

RATIONALE AND ORGANIZATION OF BOOK

This book is organized into three parts that I outline and offer rationale for here; given the critical race framework, I contextualize the work within. It is intended as more than a case study in the sociology of knowledge or an exercise in the deconstruction of dominant paradigms in mainstream criminology, although both are central to its purpose. Before I engage the current mainstream literature on racial profiling, Part I of the book originates with a grounding of history and discussion of the importance of studying racial profiling. Included is an examination of the political milieu from which racial profiling research emerged in order to give the reader context of the historical juncture that produced the contemporary works I critique. Part I also provides a contemporary as well as historical orientation for the reader to understand racial profiling processes as they manifest in the legal realm: in the analysis of chapter 2 on "Defending the Constitution?" I explore the 1996 U.S. Supreme Court decision *Whren v. United States*.[13] My discussion of the decision provides what I hope is a useful preface to the dominant narrative of citizenship and legal consciousness[14] that emerges from the qualitative analysis of in-depth interview data in Part III of the book. Briefly, the *Whren* decision, with its endorsement of the *pretextual*[15] traffic stop, provides an excellent contemporary example of law, race, and justice concerns in the post-Civil Rights era as they concern racial profiling. The *Whren* decision demonstrates the racialized practice of the state in an era where decontextualizing racial concerns has become normative, frequently through subtle discursive maneuvers. In the decision, our highest court promotes itself as concerned with racism by declaring that "the Constitution prohibits selective enforcement of the law based on considerations such as race," yet ultimately subverts the serious issue of race in a case that was inherently about race. This reflects the covert nature of racism in the post-Civil Rights era.

Part II of the book begins with chapter 3 and its critical examination of the methodology and (a)theoretical orientation (particularly its avoidance of race theory) of the current literature on racial profiling. Critical race perspectives view these as limitations because (1) an emphasis on quantification is a way to keep the public domain free of documented knowledge from historically silenced groups (if mainstream researchers do not have simple inquiries such as "what does it mean to be racially profiled?" or "what is the experience of racial profiling?" to those social actors who are central to it, our collective understanding of the phenomenon is absent a basic yet key dimension of knowledge; (2) social science has traditionally relied on quantification to support racially oppressive ideologies[16]; and (3) examinations of social phenomenon not contextualized theoretically give rise to the racial vacuum that makes up much of the racial profiling research in criminology. For example, social processes like racialized policing (as the literature currently addresses it) appear to have relatively nothing to do with racial oppression. Critical race theory is organized around the premise that race matters greatly in the social arena and any lens turned there has race at the fore. Because a primary goal of this book is to expose the *white logic* and *white methods* orientation of mainstream criminology, I devote the whole of chapter 3 to very specific criticisms of these points in the current literature that go beyond the usual review that researchers generally frame their own work within.

Part II of the book continues in chapter 4 where I offer theoretical frameworks to understand racial profiling based on my premise that racial profiling needs to be reexamined as fundamentally a process of racial oppression, especially the *everydayness* of racial oppression in the post-Civil Rights era.[17] I argue that a critical race framework is necessary to comprehend the effects of racial oppression as it manifests in racial profiling processes. To achieve this analytical goal, I incorporate theoretical perspectives on race primarily from Eduardo Bonilla-Silva, Patricia Hill Collins, W. E. B. DuBois, Joe Feagin, and Katheryn Russell. I also engage Michel Foucault's social control concept of the *panopticon* (basically, an all-seeing mechanism of the state) as it pertains to the patrolling, monitoring, and surveilling of communities of color. In chapter 5, I devote the discussion to citizenship. The citizenship realm is not engaged by mainstream racial profiling researchers to any serious degree, yet citizenship emerged as the dominant narrative in my respondents' reflections on the experience and social meaning of racial profiling. A critical race perspective is concerned with the *legal consciousness*[18] of social actors among other dimensions of the legal realm to which these concepts of social control and citizenship point.

The third and final part of the book is where I offer an analysis of qualitative data on racial profiling, including chapter 6 "An Ethnographic Reading of Racial Profiling" and chapter 7 "Vicarious Experience, Panopticonism, and Oral History."[19] I contrast the mainstream criminology orientation (quantitative heavy and atheoretical) with dominant narratives that complicate and counter much of the literature to date. Criminology, as a discipline, knows virtually nothing about what social actors subjected to racialized policing in the contemporary era experience and how they make sense of racializing and criminalizing experiences. In these final two chapters, I examine qualitatively one simple question on which the current literature is relatively silent: What is the experience of racial profiling on the social actors who are subjected to it? The qualitative approach is unique in racial profiling studies, an issue explored in-depth in chapter 3. The import of the narrative and social actors' own assessment and reflection on their lives is a defining principle of critical works. Critical race *methodology*[20] is a result of social science's historical dismissal of marginalized voices in understanding the social world. Through an examination of the narrative, our understanding of racial profiling is expanded to one not bounded by the police–minority relationship itself but one that reflects the larger political and legal realms.

My intention with this book is to push our knowledge of racial profiling into deeper, more comprehensive grounds. Because a wide-ranging critique of what comprises our current mainstream understanding is necessary in answering the call to contest the white logic of social science,[21] I detail the dominant scholarship in approach and content. I engage the racial landscape painted by traditional criminology on racial profiling by examining their methodology and theory use. Borrowing from Zuberi and Bonilla-Silva, and Young,[22] that landscape is based in a white logic orientation. This book provides an alternative portrait that engages a critical race framework. I contrast mainstream criminology approaches with the critical race approach as a way to illustrate how the dominant approach operates as a *racial project* in white criminology.[23] I argue that any understanding of racial profiling must include examination of the meanings, contexts, and assessments of these processes by the social actors who experience them. Russell, in her discussion of the out-of-place doctrine that effectively restricts autonomy of young men of color in their daily lives, states "We can only speculate as to the toll—spiritual, psychological, and physical—exacted upon a group whose freedom of movement is consistently challenged."[24] This book gets at that toll by examining the voices of those affected by the racial state practice of criminalization of, particularly, young men of color.

NOTES

1. The annual meeting of the main association of criminologists is where researchers get together to present current research. This specific reference is to the November 2003 meeting in Denver. The American Sociological Association, the main association of sociologists more generally and with which I have more experience, shares common ground here in regards to criminology-oriented sociologists' approach to the study of racial profiling.

2. The concept of race is a social construction that emerged post-fifteenth century. It is tied to European sociopolitical, geospatial expansion of religious, cultural, nationalistic, capitalist, and biological ideologies of white supremacy manifesting in social arrangements of domination and oppression. Zuberi (2001) includes the notion of "shared social experiences" in his conceptualization of race. I find this construct useful as it allies people of color as a collective in experiences with the wages of whiteness. Thus, even though there is diversity of experience among racial minority groups based on socioeconomic status, skin color, etc., the nonwhite/white dichotomy is frequently engaged in race scholarship to reflect this power differential. A related point is that social science suffers from following the black–white paradigm in race analysis, meaning that scholars tend to focus on blacks and whites, to the exclusion of other people of color, especially Asians and Native Americans (see the introduction to Brown et al. 2003 and Martinez 2007). I acknowledge this tendency in the presentation of my work here. However, because racial profiling is a relatively common experience for (young) black and Latino males, this work reflects that racial reality.

3. Basically, this refers to how the social sciences use "race" in statistical and other analyses as it were an inherent trait of the individual to which something could be ascribed, rather than the social construction that it is [AU: not a complete sentence]. Zuberi (2001) suggests that the "race effect" is a more accurate

portrayal in describing general patterns of shared social experiences delineated by phenotype. Zuberi, Tukufu. 2001. *Thicker Than Blood: How Racial Statistics Lie*. Minneapolis: University of Minnesota Press.

4. Zuberi, Tukufu, and Eduardo Bonilla-Silva. 2008. *White Logic, White Methods: Methodology and Racism*. Lanham, MD: Rowman & Littlefield.

5. Feagin, Joe R. 2006. *Systemic Racism: A Theory of Oppression*. New York: Routledge.

6. Russell, Katheryn K. 1998. *The Color of Crime: Racial Hoaxes, White Fear, Black Protectionism, Police Harassment, and Other Macroaggressions*. New York: New York University Press.

7. Russell, Katheryn K. 2001b. "Development of a Black Criminology and the Role of the Black Criminologist." Pp. 279–92 in *African American Classics in Criminology & Criminal Justice*, Shaun L. Gabbidon, Helen Taylor Greene, and Vernetta D. Young, eds. Thousand Oaks, CA: Sage Publications.

8. See, for example, Berry, Mary Frances. 1994. *Black Resistance White Law: A History of Constitutional Racism in America*. New York: Penguin Press; Haney Lopez, Ian F. 1996. *White By Law: The Legal Construction of Race*. New York: New York University Press. For a brief discussion of "dysconciousness"—a concept used in contrast to critical consciousness—see King, Joyce E. 1997. "Dysconscious Racism: Ideology, Identity, and Miseducation." Pp. 128–34 in *Critical White Studies: Looking Behind the Mirror*, Richard Delgado and Jean Stefancic, eds. Philadelphia, PA: Temple University Press.

9. Russell, Katheryn K. 1998. *The Color of Crime: Racial Hoaxes, White Fear, Black Protectionism, Police Harassment, and Other Macroaggressions*.

10. This work has particular meaning to me as it provoked a serious conflict in my graduate career when I shared it—as an act of contestation—in a course taught by a mainstream criminologist trained at a highly ranked criminology department in the United States. At that point, I knew I was on to something about the white logic practice of the discipline of criminology. Covington, Jeannette. 1995. "Racial Classification in Criminology: The Reproduction of Racialized Crime." *Sociological Forum* 10(4): 547–68. Special Issue: African Americans and Sociology: A Critical Analysis.

11. Moore, Wendy Leo. 2007. *Reproducing Racism: White Space, Elite Law Schools, and Racial Inequality*. Lanham, MD: Rowman & Littlefield.

12. Young, Vernetta D., and Helen Taylor Greene. 2000. "Pedagogical Reconstruction: Incorporating African American Perspectives into the Curriculum." Pp. 3–18 in *African American Classics in Criminology & Criminal Justice*, Shaun L. Gabbidon, Helen Taylor Greene, and Vernetta D. Young, eds. Thousand Oaks, CA: Sage.

13. *Whren v. United States*. 1996. No. 95-5841. Supreme Court of the United States. Retrieved December 14, 2004 from http://web.lexis-nexis.com/universe/printdoc.

14. Marshall, Anna-Maria, and Scott Barclay. 2003. "In Their Own Words: How Ordinary People Construct the Legal World." *Law and Social Inquiry* 28: 617–28; Nielson, Laura Beth. 2000. "Situating Legal Consciousness: Experiences and Attitudes of Ordinary Citizens about Law and Street Harassment. *Law & Society Review* 34: 1055–90.

15. *Pretextual* in the sense of useful fabrication or having another agenda.

16. Zuberi, *Thicker Than Blood.*

17. See Bonilla-Silva, Eduardo. 2003. *Racism without Racists: Color-Blind Racism and the Persistence of Racial Inequality in the United States*. Lanham, MD: Rowman & Littlefield. Feagin, Joe R. 2006. *Systemic Racism: A Theory of Oppression*. New York: Routledge.

18. Marshall, Anna-Maria, and Scott Barclay. "In Their Own Words: How Ordinary People Construct the Legal World." Nielson, "Situating Legal Consciousness."

19. See Appendix A for my methods and Appendix B for the interview schedule.

20. Solorzano, Daniel G., and Tara J. Yosso. 2002. "Critical Race Methodology: Counter-Storytelling as an Analytical Framework for Education Research." *Qualitative Inquiry* 8: 23–44.

21. Zuberi and Bonilla-Silva, *White Logic, White Methods.*

22. Zuberi and Bonnia-Silva, *White Logic, White Methods.*

23. Russell, "Development of a Black Criminology and the Role of the Black Criminologist." Omi, Michael, and Howard Winant. 1994. *Racial Formation in the United States from the 1960s to the 1990s*. New York: Routledge.

24. Russell, *Color of Crime*, p. 38.

I

1

History, Entree, and the Rise of Racial Profiling Research

HISTORY OF RACIALIZED LAW AND LAW ENFORCEMENT

Why is it important to study racial profiling? Racial profiling, considered a new phenomenon by some, is important to examine because it is actually a foundational aspect of law and law enforcement in the United States. I define racial profiling in contemporary times as the use of racial and/or ethnic status as the determinant factor in decisions to stop motorists either in the absence of indications of criminality or in determining who to enforce law against (although profiling practices encompass many social realms, my focus is its manifestation in the traffic stop, a constitutional concern over unwarranted searches and seizures). The term itself is relatively new, emerging in 1980's discourse, but the targeting of people of color by law and law enforcement is an American tradition. I begin this section with a discussion of racialized law and law enforcement to show a continuum of racial profiling policies, both informal and formal, over the centuries in the United States. Racial profiling in the contemporary era is a mere manifestation of these earlier policies.

Bonilla-Silva defines white supremacy as "racially based political regime" practices emergent post-fifteenth century that generated ideology to explain and justify racial ordering in society.[1] He contends that racism should be conceptualized in structural terms, that is, in what capacities race operates in political, social, economic, and ideological realms to establish, reinforce, and maintain racial ordering. Individuals in racialized societies such as the United States operate within social systems where some social actors are racialized as beneficiaries of white supremacy. The benefits received are various:

> the race placed in the superior position tends to receive greater economic renumeration and access to better occupations and prospects in the labor market, occupies a primary position in the political system, is granted higher social estimation (e.g., is viewed as "smarter" or "better looking" [*or non-criminal*]), often has the license to draw physical (segregation) as well as social (racial etiquette) boundaries between itself and other races, and receives what W. E. B. DuBois called a "psychological wage."[2]

The practices of racialized social systems and frameworks to facilitate the racial arrangements in society are dynamic temporally. Each racial group develops its own interest and practice in preserving or contesting the racial order. Over time, as racial contestation increases, legal and extralegal practices force a movement toward more covert forms of racialized law from the racial state.[3] Such movement from overt to covert social practices is expected in the era of color-blind racism.[4]

Russell lays out a timeline of racialized law and racialized law enforcement, starting with the arrival of the first slave ship in 1619 Virginia and the resulting *slave codes*.[5] Slave codes socially controlled Africans and African Americans from birth to even after death. Color distinctions—the "degree of blackness" one was assumed to possess—was formalized into the law, with those ranked *white* receiving the greatest protections under the law.[6] The legal reasoning of the "one-drop rule" of hypodescent (an accounting of perceived blood quantum) meant that there were only two racial categories, white and nonwhite. Slave codes regulated racial status first, with behavioral considerations a secondary aspect of the decrees. Thus, a fundamental aspect of the law that founded colonial America and the United States was based solely on the regulation of the racialized body.

Assaults, rapes, and murders, among other deviant behaviors, were assessed for punishment depending on who the offender was and/or who the victim was *racially*, thus establishing a pattern of racialized social control from the earliest times of colonial America. Russell views the "slave patrols" that emerged during this time as the "first uniquely American form of policing," explaining:

> Slave patrols . . . operated to keep a tight rein on slave activity. Whites greatly feared slave insurrection and the slave patrols were established to monitor and quell suspicious slave conduct. . . . Slave patrollers, who worked in conjunction with the militia, were permitted to stop, search, and beat slaves who did not have proper permission to be away from their plantation. Whites in every community were enlisted to participate in the patrols. In Alabama, for example, all slave owners under age 60 and all other Whites under age 45

> were legally required to perform slave patrol duties. By the mid-1850s, slave patrols existed in every Southern colony.[7]

This emphasis on the regulation of the body and social space is clearly a defining characteristic of current racial profiling processes. The "white-boy-in-a-no-white-boy-zone" phenomenon[8] is a contemporary manifestation of keeping communities of color on "their plantation." The *out-of-place doctrine* that some today view as good policing is normative in police–minority relations and dates back to these earlier eras of overt racialized state social control.

A civil war theoretically over the abolishment of the institution of slavery did not end official racialization processes in the United States, nor did it end covert racial policies of the state. With abolition in 1865, the slave codes that regulated race relations in colonial America through the presidency of Lincoln were struck down, yet white interests were maintained with the establishment of the black codes that same year.[9] As described by Joe Feagin:[10]

> The economic exploitation of slavery was replaced under segregation by the near-slavery of sharecropping, tenant farming, debt peonage, and low-paid manual or domestic work. Almost all better paying jobs outside black communities were off-limits to African Americans. Whites generally benefited from higher wages, as well as from the exclusion of black workers from many jobs in workplaces and businesses. Segregation significantly reduced job competition for white workers.

MAINTAINING TWO SOCIOLEGAL REALMS: OVERTLY AND COVERTLY

The legal realm was also readjusted to accommodate the changing social arrangements in the antebellum period. The construction of two legal systems, one for whites and one for *others*, was well established by the time separate but equal legislation became formal with the 1896 *Plessy v. Ferguson* U.S. Supreme Court decision.[11] In formal capacity, these so-called Jim Crow statutes facilitated white supremacy until the late 1960s. As stated by Russell, "One constant remained as the slave codes became the black codes and the black codes became segregation statutes: Blackness itself was a crime."[12]

After nearly three centuries of overtly racialized law in America, *Plessy* signaled one of the earliest moves toward "color-blind racism" from the U.S. Supreme Court. The Court discursively engaged notions of equality as stated in the Constitution and other forms of legislation, ostensibly color blind to the inequity that surrounded them.[13] Yet the racialized milieu that supported those centuries of blatant racialization and criminalization processes would preside over any formal discursive changes made by the Court. As Moore observes, even at the highest levels of the state, there was tacit recognition of the racial reality that law, however bold in its assertions, is only as effective as the enforcement and practices of its application:[14]

> Racial group boundaries were constructed to separate and denote substantive difference, and the construction and maintenance of racial difference in the United States was at no time separate from the enforcement of racial oppression. The "separate but equal" doctrine was, from its inception, a lie. The facilities created to keep African Americans separate from whites were never "equal" in any sense of the word, as the courts and state were well aware. And in fact, just moments after suggesting that the legal differentiation between whites and African Americans did not have the effect of denying legal equality, the Court recognized that it was perpetuating racial subjugation saying,
>
> > *The object of the {Fourteenth Amendment} was undoubtedly to enforce the absolute equality of the two races before the law, but in the nature of things, it could not have been intended to abolish distinctions based upon color, or to enforce social, as distinguished from political, equality, or a commingling of the two races.*
>
> Thus, the Court suggested that the equality of which the justices spoke was restricted to "political equality" and certainly did not include "social" equality; as such, it recognized the legally protected right of white people to engage in racism.

The U.S. Supreme Court's 1954 *Brown v. Board of Education* provided some hope as it was one of the first in a series of legal doctrines taking deliberate discursive measures toward racial equality. Yet the social control efforts—both informal and formal—to maintain practices of racialized social space persisted. In later years, the Civil Rights Act of 1964 and the Voting Rights Act of 1965 ushered in more formalization of legal discourse that would be discursively useful in the emergence of colorblind racism in the years to come. When social forces bring change to the particular form of a given racialized social system, it is unlikely that the social system becomes far removed from racialization processes as such alternatives are not available.[15] The timeline of racialized law informs this argument: With the abolition of slavery came not a nonracialized society but a society racialized in a different context and practice.

The racist law and law enforcement that governed colonial America consistently subsumed different forms over the years yet remains a fundamental legal arrangement in the United States. Changes in the racial structure of racial social systems occur when racial conflict—from both dominant and subordinate groups—forces it.[16] The post-Civil Rights era, with color-blind racism as its most common form (though not exclusive form) of racism, is no different. Racial profiling, with its tricky operations and handy discursive strategies at hand for justification, is one of the main forms racialized law has taken in the contemporary era.

Yet, mainstream criminology's treatment of racial profiling does not contextualize and rarely acknowledges in depth this social fact of racism in the United States. When mainstream criminology does discuss racism, it is generally framed as a historical artifact with waning influence in contemporary times. Mainstream criminology perpetuates racial inequality in the United States by continuing to establish, reinforce, and perpetuate the association of criminality and minority racial status. In chapter 3, I analyze the treatment of racial profiling by mainstream criminology to demonstrate the discursive strategies and special effects this white logic framework uses in support of the racial structure of the United States.

RACIAL PROFILING AS ENTREE TO THE CRIMINAL JUSTICE SYSTEM

Another compelling reason to examine racial profiling is its capacity to usher young men of color into the criminal justice system, a system racially ordered in many aspects.[17] Criminology traditionally focuses on formal stages of the criminal justice system such as sentencing and parole. However, the informal stages of criminal justice are increasingly important areas of examination if we are to understand the more subtle mechanisms that play a large role in who gets introduced to the criminal justice system. Racial profiling is a fundamental step in *prearrest contacts*, and accordingly, "these encounters, which are not subject to official measure, must be included in an assessment of whether the justice system operates in a racially biased manner."[18] This historical tendency of mainstream criminology to focus on the formal stages when informal processes such as racial profiling are highly influential in shaping the hue of the criminal justice system is reflective of the white logic orientation of the social sciences.[19] As well, formal modes of social control overtly racialized in earlier times have evolved into less formal practices that may be more difficult—or "tricky" as one respondent labeled it—to detect, particularly when social science engages the same methodologies, theories, and inquiries employed in those earlier eras.

Russell's call from a decade ago to examine the informal processes of the criminal justice system (processes facilitated by engagement of the *criminalblackman* stereotype) was not foretelling of the type of research focus that would emerge however, in part because of the lack of critical theory employed in traditional criminology. This book presents an opportunity to see what can be learned about racial profiling when examined outside of the white logic lens of traditional criminology. Because a critical race framework is interested in the racial epoch from which particularly *political* scholarship arises, I briefly discuss here the emergence of racial profiling research.

THE RISE OF RACIAL PROFILING RESEARCH

The political context of the emergence of racial profiling research is important to acknowledge. I identify three social conditions that set the stage for the rise of racial profiling research. To start, the first of several lawsuits was initiated by motorists of color fed up with racialized policing practices and who turned to the courts for remedy.[20] The first lawsuit led to what many consider the first study on racial profiling, led by John Lamberth.[21] A second condition that facilitated the research agenda was the tumultuous times following the brutal beating of Rodney King in 1991. The ensuing riots and public discourse about police brutality included the broader notion of racialized policing. Both of these social conditions seemed to bode well for critics of racial profiling who were demanding state accountability in the legal (lawsuits are an example of working in the system for justice) and public (riots are an example of working outside of the system) realms.

The third condition, I argue, may explain the inherent white logic orientation of mainstream criminology on racial profiling—the public discourse and state practice surrounding high rates of crime in the 1980s and early 1990s. In actuality, only coming into its own as scholarship in the mid-1990s, research on racial profiling came on the heels of a decade characterized by high rates of drug and violence-related crime, accompanying hypercriminalization of young black men, a movement concerned with the need to recover from the "lost generation" of black men, and injection of specified discourse about young men of color that included the concept of "wilding"—criminal violence rampages by *animalized* youth of color referred to as "superpredators."[22]

The increasing crime control model orientation encompassed in "zero tolerance" and "broken windows theory" policing was in full bloom during this period.[23] Discursively promoted as "quality-of-life" policies, these law enforcement strategies were based on the idea that small infractions of the social order, if not sanctioned by the state, would give way to large, more dangerous violations. These quality-of-life policies, however, received some degree of public heat for their disproportionate application to the poor and communities of color.

The commonsense nature of racial profiling that underlies the *rational discrimination* argument suggests that targeting young males of color makes sense given the hue of the criminal justice system; this white logic orientation may have also fertilized the scholarly ground for the emergence of the scholarship. As Alford Young[24] states:

> The 1980s was a period of sweeping public exposure to and rapid acceptance of the concept of the underclass. This term was used in social scientific inquiry and policy circles to designate a segment of the urban poor as a criminally inclined, violence-prone, and culturally deficient group of individuals who were locked in an inescapable web of economic deprivation and pathology.

Furthermore, Young examines the tradition of ethnographic studies by white researchers in the 1960s and how it focused on "white understandings" of a deficit-based black community but argues that more recent ethnography by white scholars in the 1990s "was rooted in a national condition of intense anxiety about the presumably extreme threat to the American social order that such people represented."[25] Both treatments—that of pathology and that of threat—provide context for the racial profiling research emerging in the 1990s.

Although racial profiling research emerged from the Rodney King events and motorists of color turning to the courts for a remedy to unconstitutional seizures by the state, the rise of it to the top of the criminology research agenda in the 1990s, I argue, suggests that the milieu that Young describes—a (white) national concern about the "extreme threat" posed by young men of color in particular—is the more compelling reason for the rise of the agenda. Simultaneously, the criminalizing discourse surrounding young men of color weakened any nominal resistance to not using racial status as a signifier of criminality in social control practices by the racial state. If the research was viewed as legitimate by those in the public domain, then the racial profiling "makes sense to me" argument (rational discrimination) could be used more overtly in shaping state policy on crime control. Where might we turn to show evidence of this allegation? The legislative fallout and dominant discourses following September 11, 2001, provides a compelling example.

I have laid out a context for possible reasons why racial profiling research took off at the historical juncture that it did, considering communities of color have been voicing opposition to racialized social control practices for centuries. The next point to briefly address is the emphasis on quantitative methods that made up the bulk of research, a subject I explore more in depth in chapter 3.

Claims of racial profiling by communities of color were met with the common response that there were no scientific data to support the claims, only anecdotal evidence.[26] There was no proof that racial profiling existed—the numbers were just not there. The studies that make up the first wave of research on racial profiling—those studies examining racial status disproportionality and officer decision-making processes, for instance—quickly dismantled this argument. Now the numbers *were* there and they overwhelmingly showed racial disparity in traffic stops.[27] As the numbers of these disproportionate-oriented studies grew, researchers responded to claims that the baselines (the denominators) used to determine disproportionality in the early studies were flawed. These critiques reflect not only a determination to get the methods right, but given the lack of attention directed to mainstream criminology about the social effects of racialized policing on communities of color (evident by their neglect in studying the social actors subjected to the phenomenon), they may also be viewed as reluctance to accept the conclusions offered by these studies, that is, that racialized policing is a fundamental practice of the racial state.[28] More and more sophisticated baseline strategies were introduced, applied to more and more sophisticated data collections, yet the general conclusion that people of color were stopped disproportionately, relative to white motorists, remained the same.

At this point, the quantitative emphasis by racial profiling researchers may be considered, from a critical race theory perspective, what Michael Omi and Howard Winant term a *racial project*: "simultaneously an interpretation, representation, or explanation of racial dynamics, and an effort to reorganize and redistribute resources along particular racial lines."[29] Critical race frameworks implore researchers to examine, among other things, what and how inquiries are being made, who is being asked about a phenomenon, and how the phenomenon is being measured or defined. A dominant methodology that defines a field of research, from a critical race framework, signals neglect in considering alternatives and a disinterest in thinking outside the box of white logic to provide counterknowledge of the issue at hand. Qualitative work provides voices that can inform us about the processes and meanings of the racial status quo. Because criminology is traditionally centered on social control and less about the sociology of law, it makes sense that the methodology dominating the discipline and the field of racial profiling research fits politically.

On the occasions where racial profiling researchers claim to include the perspectives of the citizens in their studies, it is often in the form of survey-driven research noting attitudes toward law enforcement across racial groups. This orientation is a reflection of the traditional view of examining race relations as about individual attitudes and less about systemic operations of white supremacy ideology. Among the problems with attitudinal research emphases are the Likert-scale formulations that force respondents into a small range of possible responses that then are useful only relative to other demographic response levels.[30] For example, attitudinal research reinforces the white-framed mythology that communities of color have an anti-law and order position as reflected by their weak showing of support for law enforcement, relative to whites' support. While this offers a sense of the experiences of different groups, it is also a good illustration that high levels of support for a social institution likely means that that system works for you. When social institutions do not work as they should (it should be the case that the criminal justice system operates fairly), people are not supportive.

CONCLUSION

Claims of racial progress in the United States are frequently embedded in discourse that engages as "the past is the past" storyline.[31] Whites and some people of color point to the virtual lack of overtly racialized law—for example, Jim Crow statutes—in efforts to paint the operation of law and law enforcement in the contemporary era as relatively neutral. Yet critical examination of law and law enforcement demonstrates a myriad of processes that further the tradition of racialized law in the United States. As discussed in this opening chapter, when systems of oppression are challenged, they have historically *reorganized*. Mainstream criminology, by distancing itself from in-depth analysis of race, neglects these reorganizations and racial realities even when examining concerns that are, I argue, inherently about race.

In the next chapter I discuss one of the defining reorganizations of racialized law in the contemporary era—the U.S. Supreme Court decision *Whren v. United States* in 1996. Going to the roots of a critical race theory framework, the following discussion illuminates the subtle discursive and practical turns of race, law, and justice as they concern the *pretextual* traffic stop and its place in contemporary racialized law enforcement processes.

NOTES

1. Bonilla-Silva, Eduardo. 2003. *Racism without Racists: Color-Blind Racism and the Persistence of Racial Inequality in the United States*. Lanham, MD: Rowman & Littlefield, p. 11.
2. Bonilla-Silva, *Racism without Racists*, p. 37.
3. Omi, Michael, and Howard Winant. 1994. *Racial Formation in the United States from the 1960s to the 1990s*. New York: Routledge.
4. Bonilla-Silva, *Racism without Racists*.

5. Russell, Katheryn K. 1998. *The Color of Crime: Racial Hoaxes, White Fear, Black Protectionism, Police Harassment, and Other Macroaggressions*. New York: New York University Press.

6. Russell, *The Color of Crime*. Berry, Mary Frances. 1994. *Black Resistance, White Law: A History of Constitutional Racism in America*. New York: Penguin Press.

7. Russell, *The Color of Crime*, p. 18.

8. A reference to a now-defunct police radio call that demonstrates the salience of race and social space. Glover, Karen S. 2007. "Police Discourse on Racial Profiling." *Journal of Contemporary Criminal Justice* 23: 239–47.

9. Berry, *Black Resistance, White Law*.

10. Feagin, Joe R. 2006. *Systemic Racism: A Theory of Oppression*. New York: Routledge, p. 150.

11. Fireside, Harvey. 2004. *Separate and Unequal: Homer Plessy and the Supreme Court Decision that Legalized Racism*. New York: Carroll & Graf Publishers.

12. Russell, *The Color of Crime*, p. 22.

13. Bell, Derrick. 2000. *Race, Racism, and American Law*. New York. Aspen Publishers.

14. Moore, Wendy L. 2007. *Reproducing Racism: White Space, Elite Law Schools, and Racial Inequality*. Lanham, MD: Rowman & Littlefield.

15. Bonilla-Silva, *Racism without Racists*.

16. Bonilla-Silva, *Racism without Racists*.

17. Berry, *Black Resistance, White Law*. Covington, Jeannette. 2001. "Round Up the Usual Suspects: Racial Profiling and the War on Drugs." Pp. 27–42 in *Petit Apartheid in the U.S. Criminal Justice System: The Dark Figure of Racism*, Dragan Milovanovic and Katheryn K. Russell, eds. Durham, NC: Carolina Academic Press; Pettit, Becky, and Bruce Western. 2004. "Mass Imprisonment and the Life Course: Race and Class Inequality in U.S. Incarceration." *American Sociological Review* 69: 151–69. Gabbidon, Shaun L., Helen Taylor Greene, and Vernetta D. Young, eds. 2002. *African American Classics in Criminology & Criminal Justice*. Thousand Oaks, CA: Sage Publications.

18. Russell, *The Color of Crime*, p. 32.

19. Zuberi, Tukufu, and Eduardo Bonilla-Silva. 2008. *White Logic, White Methods: Racism and Methodology*. Lanham, MD: Rowman & Littlefield.

20. Withrow, Brian L. 2006. *Racial Profiling: From Rhetoric to Reason*. Upper Saddle River, NJ: Pearson-Prentice Hall.

21. Lamberth, John. 1998. *Driving While Black: A Statistician Proves That Prejudice Still Rules the Road*. Retrieved September 3, 2002. www.hartford-hwp.com/archives/45a/192.html.

22. Bennett, William J., John J. Diilulio, and John P. Walters. 1996. *Body Count: Moral Poverty . . . and How to Win America's War against Crime and Drugs*. New York: Simon & Schuster.

23. Harcourt, Bernard E. 2001. *Illusion of Order: The False Promise of Broken Windows Policing*. Cambridge, MA: Harvard University Press.

24. Young, Alford. 2008. "White Ethnographers on the Experiences of African American Men: Then and Now." Pp. 179–200 in *White Logic, White Methods: Racism and Methodology*, Tukufu Zuberti and Eduardo Bonilla-Silva, eds. Lanham, MD: Rowman & Littlefield, p. 187.

25. Young, "White Ethnographers on the Experiences of African American Men," p. 180.
26. Withrow, *Racial Profiling*.
27. Withrow, *Racial Profiling*.
28. See Omi and Winant for analysis of state practices that establish and maintain the racial order in the United States. Omi and Winant, *Racial Formation in the United States from the 1960s to the 1990s*.
29. Omi and Winant, *Racial Formation in the United States from the 1960s to the 1990s*, p. 56.
30. Russell, *The Color of Crime*.
31. Bonilla-Silva, *Racism without Racists*.

2

Defending the Constitution?

The right of the people to be secure in their persons, houses, papers, and effects, against unreasonable searches and seizures, shall not be violated, and no Warrants shall issue, but upon probable cause, supported by Oath or affirmation, and particularly describing the place to be searched, and the persons or things to be seized.

—Fourth Amendment to the U.S. Constitution

Section 1. All persons born or naturalized in the United States and subject to the jurisdiction thereof, are citizens of the United States and of the State wherein they reside. No State shall make or enforce any law which shall abridge the privileges or immunities of citizens of the United States; nor shall any State deprive any person of life, liberty, or property, without due process of law; nor deny to any person within its jurisdiction the equal protection of the laws.

—Fourteenth Amendment to the U.S. Constitution

In a "high drug area" of Washington, D.C., officers in an unmarked police car observed a darkened Pathfinder with temporary tags at a stop sign. Officers noticed that the vehicle was stopped at the intersection for 20 or more seconds, an unusual amount of time to be stopped according to the police report. Its youthful black occupants included the driver, Brown, who was observed looking down at the lap of the passenger, Whren. The officers turned around to head toward the vehicle and observed it make a "sudden" right turn without signaling, after which it sped off at "unreasonable" speed. The police pulled up behind the vehicle at a red traffic signal. One officer quickly approached the occupants and observed two large bags of what appeared to be crack cocaine in passenger Whren's hands. The two were arrested on drug charges.

The petitioners challenged the legality of the stop at the district court level, arguing that there was not *probable cause* (a reference to Fourth Amendment protections) or *reasonable suspicion* (a reference to the *Terry v. Ohio* decision by the U.S. Supreme Court that effectively lowered the standard of constitutionality on state intervention)—two earlier standards applied to search and seizure cases—to infer that they were doing anything illegal. As such, the officer's claim that he approached them to offer a warning about the traffic violations (staying at a stop sign for a lengthy period of time, not signaling a turn, and driving away at an unreasonable speed) was a *pretext* for discovering contraband such as illegal drugs or weapons. The petitioners, both of whom were black, contend that the police might use race as a factor when deciding which motorists to make a traffic stop on—that the probable cause standard to suspect criminality was indeed the color of their skin.

This chapter concerns how the legal realm facilitates the social reproduction of racial inequality in the contemporary era. I focus on the 1996 U.S. Supreme Court decision *Whren v. United States* because of its centrality to racial profiling processes both discursively and in practice.[1] In many respects, racial profiling discourse was at a peak in the early 1990s following the not-guilty verdicts for the Los Angeles Police Department officers indicted for the brutal beating of motorist Rodney King in 1991. Although the term racial profiling is a relatively contemporary expression in the discourse of police–minority relations, the practices of the state to attribute criminality to racial minority status is nothing new. The defendants in *Whren* basically argued that they were racially profiled. This case, with that as its defining if not always proclaimed characteristic, made it all the way to the United States Supreme Court!

The contemporary era is characterized by the dominant racial ideology of color-blind racism in which, for instance, one rationalizes, operates within, and maintains the racial order in seemingly nonracial ways.[2] The *Whren* case established an excellent example of how important judicial decisions—the formal legal workings in our racial social system—operate in conjunction with dominant racial ideology to facilitate racial oppression. The *Whren* decision effectively enforces the practice of racial profiling by granting constitutional coverage to the *pretextual* traffic stop. The pretextual stop is a strategy engaged by law enforcement when an officer stops a motorist for what might be a very minor violation of the traffic code under *pretext* (having another agenda, useful fabrication) in order to have access to the motorist and vehicle that the officer is suspicious of but about whom the officer cannot establish *probable cause* or articulate *reasonable suspicion* (again, two earlier standards of conduct for state intervention).

To bolster their complaint of unfair practices by the state, the petitioners argued that regulations for the District of Columbia police department include code that plainclothes officers in an unmarked police car can enforce traffic laws only under particular conditions (graveness, threats to others) that were not present during the petitioners' stop. As noted in one law review journal, the absence of these regulation conditions indicates that "there is little doubt that their conduct was not what a reasonable officer in their department would do, at least assuming that a reasonable officer follows regulations."[3]

The district court denied the challenge and the petitioners were convicted of the drug charges. The appeals court affirmed the decision, stating "regardless of whether a police officer subjectively believes that the occupants of an automobile may be engaging in some other illegal behavior, a traffic stop is permissible as long as a *reasonable* officer in the same circumstances *could have* stopped the car for the suspected traffic violation."[4] The temporary detention of individuals during a traffic stop, even for a brief time and without a citation being issued, is considered a seizure under Fourth Amendment guarantees of protection against unreasonable searches and seizures. Traffic stops are subject to constitutional protections against police intrusion of motorists. "Reasonable" seizures are those that balance well governmental interests with the weight of the intrusions suffered upon the individual's privacy.

Yet both of these lower court decisions supported state social control practices, with the appeal court decision clearly acknowledging the subjectivity of the officers' original suspicions to monitor motorist Brown and passenger Whren. More importantly, the origins of the Fourth Amendment emerged from a concern over governmental abuse of power as it applies to the British authorities and their practices of using writs of ill to control the colonists. The founders of colonial America—themselves opposed to unwarranted state intervention because of their experiences with it—with the adoption of the Bill of Rights (the first ten Constitutional Amendments) made clear that the highest law in the land would offer protections against unwarranted searches and seizures by the state.

In the era of color-blind racism, the decision reflects a contemporary failure of the U.S. Supreme Court to live up to its role as a protector of constitutional rights in the United States. In a clearly color-blind racism fashion, the *Whren* decision dismissed the salience of race in contemporary times and established greater latitude for police powers that have been used historically and contemporarily to oppress communities of color.

As support for this contention, I point to the brevity of the Court's acknowledgment of race in a decision that was inherently about racism. It came in a single reference that directed the *Whren* complaint to potential review as a Fourteenth Amendment, rather than Fourth Amendment, case. Fourteenth Amendment cases are notoriously difficult to litigate because of the strict standards of proof of intent and disparity. At the height of public concern about racial profiling following the Rodney King beating, the U.S. Supreme Court's 1996 decision in *Whren* reinforced the dominant paradigm of social regulation by race under the purview of the street cop.

In deconstructions of the *Whren* decision, legal scholars have framed it as a standard of "could have" versus "would have."[5] The former refers to the police officer's ability to legally make the traffic stop after observation of a traffic violation. The stricter standard that the *Whren* decision dismissed is the latter scenario—basically an examination of police discretion and regular practice that a reasonable police officer would or would not engage. The pretextual stop, under the *could have* ruling in *Whren* permits a racially motivated officer to make the traffic stop legally when an officer operating without keen racial motivation perhaps would not have made the stop. The ultimate question is, since the *Whren* decision allows the police to legally stop anyone driving a car if it is observed making one of the ever-present violations of the traffic code, who will the police stop? In a racially ordered society, the answer is clear. Thus, the *Whren* decision serves as a contemporary example of color-blind racism at the highest levels of our legal system because of the justices' lack of regard for the racialized mileu in which their decision will take effect.

The key part of *Whren* that makes its reach so pervasive is the omnipresence of the traffic violation. As argued in *Whren*, the control of vehicles is strictly regulated to the point that minute code violations are made with great regularity by almost all drivers. Officers subjectively suspicious of the occupants of a vehicle need only follow that vehicle until a minor violation occurs before they can legally pull the vehicle over. *Whren*, when given this bevy of available violations, however inconsequential, provides the police officer with legal grounds to make a stop, regardless of the motivation that alerted the officer on the motorist originally. In a racially ordered society such as the United States, the considerable police discretion allowed by *Whren* presents an obvious concern for racial justice.

At the heart of the *Whren* decision is whether subjective intentions that motivated a legal traffic stop are held up in regards to the legal concept of *discovery*. Discovery refers to the evidence that is used against a defendant in a court of law: evidence collected illegally will not be permitted in that court of law. Thus, if racial profiling is considered an illegal practice because of constitutional protections against unreasonable searches and seizures, evidence collected during a racial profiling stop is not admissible in a court of law. The *Whren* decision effectively eliminates constitutional consideration of unreasonableness (in searches and seizures) because it places the objective findings of the traffic stop, perhaps a very minor infraction of the traffic code, as the sole distinction in determining the legality of a traffic stop.

Under *Whren*, if an officer makes a traffic stop of a young black male based on a minor code infraction because of an assumption that young black males are likely to be involved in criminal activity, and if indeed the officer finds contraband during the stop, the minor code infraction effectively trumps the racial discrimination that led to the stop in the first place. In the *Whren* decision, the justices speak of the "subjectivity" of knowing the officer's intent, and argue that the constitutional reasonableness of the stops, when based on an actual violation, is not determined based on the individual motivations of the officer involved. A legal instructor at the FBI Academy wrote[6]:

> The implications of the *Whren* decision for law enforcement are numerous. First, it maintains consistency in the Supreme Court's decisions interpreting the Fourth Amendment standard of "reasonableness" as being objective, thus precluding consideration of an officer's subjective motivation. Second, the *Whren* decision continues to permit officer discretion in the enforcement of traffic and other relatively minor violations. By virtue of their volume and nature, minor infractions of the law are less compelling of law enforcement time and resources than more serious offenses; consequently, their enforcement must, of necessity, be somewhat selective and discretionary.

When race is removed from judicial examinations of traffic stop practices, the decision by the court seems relatively benign. The FBI legal instructor praises the affirmation of the Court that the subjective considerations that may lead to a traffic stop are excluded if objective reasoning is uncovered. "Reason" and objectiveness form the criteria for a decision that is largely examined as one based on rational behavior, not racial discrimination and thus fits nicely with post-Civil Rights racial discourse.[7] The virtually unlimited objective data, that is, the minor traffic infractions that normally occur while driving with most motorists, are partnered with an understanding that discretion is part of the process, and thus, normalized. As in much of the post-Civil Rights discourse about the significance of race in society, the mandatory clause expressing concern for racial equality appears somewhat dismissively. The FBI legal instructor comments on the importance of noting that "the Supreme Court's decision in *Whren* is not a signal for law enforcement officers to become arbitrary and capricious in deciding when to make a Fourth Amendment search or seizure."[8] Another FBI analysis of the pretextual stop explained[9]:

> In reality, however, determining the reasonableness of a seizure can be an extremely difficult task. No mathematical or scientific formula exists for predicting when facts and circumstances rise to the level of reasonable suspicion

or probable cause; yet, law enforcement officers are required to make such judgments on a daily basis and act on them. Once acted upon, those judgments are subject to seemingly endless defense challenges.

Others in the debate over these legal protections and racial profiling view the profiling controversy in harsher terms but do not deny that racial profiling exists. Police studies scholars Buerger and Farrell capture this aspect of the debate neatly[10]:

> From the police standpoint, racial profiling is a media invention, a distorting label used by self-serving antipolice individuals against the hard-working police officers tend to personify this fear in the persons of Jesse Jackson and Al Sharpton, or in their local counterparts, persons whose activism against police abuses—real or perceived—has earned the enmity of a substantial number of officers. . . . Nevertheless, the term strikes a resounding chord with thousands of citizens of minority status whose direct and vicarious experiences confirm that such a practice does exist and is a daily reality in their lives.

Yet, the problem is clear: the *Whren* decision provides law enforcement with the legal capacity to make subjective stops if objective grounds are successfully sought out. Placed in the context of a racially ordered society such as the United States, the ramifications of subjectively based policing will greatly impact communities of color.

EQUAL PROTECTION CLAUSE

Some interpret the language of the *Whren* decision as a direct call from the Court that they will consider a challenge to the use of race in policing if a case is brought up under the Fourteenth Amendment.[11] The *Whren* decision is even invoked, mistakenly, as a safeguard against racial discrimination in this reply from the U.S. Assistant Attorney General and Assistant Secretary of State to the United Nations Committee on the Elimination of Racial Discrimination. When asked what the United States was doing about concerns with racism in the criminal justice system, they responded:[12]

> The Supreme Court has already held that what we recently have come to refer to in America as "racial profiling" is unconstitutional. In *Whren v. United States* (1996), the Court stated with a unanimous voice that "the Constitution prohibits selective enforcement of the law based on considerations such as race" under the Equal Protection Clause of the Fourteenth Amendment. The Fourteenth Amendment applies to all of our 50 states.

More critical scholars examine the same language and regard it as "dismissing" the practice of racially based law enforcement.[13] The passing off of the race issue to Fourteenth Amendment considerations has its own problems, as described by Angela J. Davis:[14]

> An African-American motorist alleging that a police officer's use of a pretextual traffic stop constituted a denial of equal protection would need to show that similarly situated white motorists could have been stopped, detained or arrested, but were not. Armstrong *[reference to a court decision establishing standards of discovery in selective prosecution cases]* suggests that they would need to provide some evidence of such failures to stop to obtain discovery and presumably more of such evidence to prevail on the merits. How could a motorist obtain such evidence? Even if he did not have to cross the Armstrong hurdle to get discovery, such information would not be readily available. Police officers do not keep records of instances in which they could have stopped a motorist for a traffic violation, but did not.

As such, the court's reliance on the Fourteenth Amendment to be the guard against racially discriminatory policing is a mute point, given the strict standard established by *Armstrong*. This social fact reflects how the color-blind racism of the Court manifests in key decisions concerning racialized law enforcement.

Racially discriminatory policing has been described as possessing two primary components.[15] First, police treatment of "visible" racial minorities is inferior to the police treatment of similarly situated whites. For example, a minority who is stopped on a minor traffic infraction may be issued a ticket while a white offender is only issued a warning. Second, the situation where a person is targeted for police attention based on his/her race or ethnicity and not based on behavior or violation of law. Cooper maintains that consequences of the *Whren* decision will "exacerbate the epidemic of racially discriminatory policing."[16]

Police researchers Milazzo and Hansen comment that the matter of profiling seems only to be objectionable when minorities are linked to drug-related crimes, citing the apparently noncontroversial association of white male status with serial killing, arson, and child molestation.[17] They argue that for racial minorities and whites, "arrest and conviction statistics provide an empirical basis for inclusion in a profile."[18] The cycle is vicious: People of color, particularly young black males, are profiled as being involved in the drug trade by law enforcement and thus the empirical basis, e.g., the arrest and conviction statistics, reinforce the profile when in fact it may be motivated in large part out of racial bias and criminalization processes.

Whren may be viewed as "more than a missed opportunity for the Court to rein in some police practices that strike at the heart of the ideas of freedom and equal treatment; *Whren* represents a clear step in the other direction—toward authoritarianism, toward racist policing, and toward a view of minorities as criminals, rather than citizens."[19] The Court's direction that the case would be more appropriate as a Fourteenth Amendment case is nullified when considering the results of Equal Protection cases such as *McCleskey v. Kemp* (described below) that offered impotent remedies for racial discrimination in the criminal justice system. Davis warns that the *Whren* decision leaves people of color "without an effective remedy for discriminatory pretextual traffic stops" when the Court offers up the Equal Protection Clause as protection.[20]

As discussed above, the Court suggested that the Equal Protection Clause of the Fourteenth Amendment was the more appropriate legal maneuver to argue for the *Whren* complaint. As follows, this single reference is the extent of the Court's specific engagement of race, even though it was the essential argument of the plaintiffs' case:[21]

> We of course agree with petitioners that the Constitution prohibits selective enforcement of the law based on considerations such as race. But the constitutional basis for objecting to intentionally discriminatory application of laws is the Equal Protection Clause, not the Fourth Amendment. Subjective intentions play no role in ordinary, probable-cause Fourth Amendment analysis.

Another example of how the highest court in the land operates in the era of color-blind racism[22] is discussed by Russell in *The Color of Crime*.[23] She cites the case of *McCleskey v. Kemp* in which a black murder defendant argued that the death penalty was racially biased and in violation of the Fourteenth Amendment's Equal Protection Clause. To demonstrate, a study of the Georgia death penalty system showing a race-of-victim effect was introduced to the Court: While only 1 percent of murder cases involving a black offender and a black victim resulted in the death penalty, 22 percent of the cases involving a black offender and a white victim resulted in the death penalty. The U.S. Supreme Court did not deny that the racial disparity existed but maintained that each death penalty case had to show that the sentence was motivated by racial bias. This high standard is particularly difficult to meet, as individuals (jurors, judges, etc.) living in the era of color-blind racism would be hesitant to admit racial animus openly. In this instance, the failure of the Court to establish a legal remedy for the institutional pattern of racism inherent in the death penalty system in effect supports the discrimination by omission. As suggested by critical race scholar Davis, this decision "strikes the black reader of law as microaggression—stunning, automatic acts of disregard that stem from unconscious attitudes of white superiority and constitute a verification of black inferiority."[24]

This is not to say that the Court did not acknowledge some problems with the *Whren* decision, as they included language about possible ill effects of *Whren*:[25]

> petitioners point out that our cases acknowledge that even ordinary traffic stops entail "a possibly unsettling show of authority"; that they at best "interfere with freedom of movement, are inconvenient, and consume time" and at worst "may create substantial anxiety" . . . that anxiety is likely to be even more pronounced when the stop is conducted by plainclothes officers in unmarked cars.

Law enforcement insiders have acknowledged the burden of racially discriminatory policing on people of color. Following the *Whren* decision, a meeting of the International Association of Chiefs of Police (IACP) included a comment on the effects of *Whren* from police researchers:[26]

> The Court ruled consistently with historical interpretations of the Fourth Amendment, deciding that an officer's subjective intention is irrelevant in determining whether there is objective factual justification for a vehicle stop. Despite the constitutionality of the practice, motorists understand that they are being stopped for a different reason than the one provided and are angered by the inference needed to make the stop. . . . As more anecdotal stories circulate about such stops, the long-term effect on race relations must be balanced against the short-term effect on drug enforcement.

Simply acknowledging these harms in the wake of a decision as meaningful as *Whren*, however, is not enough. Russell offers *affirmative race law* in response to racial inequality in the criminal justice system.[27] As briefly discussed in the introductory chapter, affirmative race law is that legislation that seeks to address overt and covert racial discrimination by acknowledging the troubled history of the United States, the racist foundation of the criminal justice system, and the potential social harm that future generations may experience if the current system is not changed. Affirmative race law is concerned with both the laws that are currently in place and with the law that can be established in the criminal justice system to thwart racial discrimination. A critique of affirmative race law is that it merely creates *more* law that will likely be reinforced differentially. What is the state of affairs with legislation—affirmative race law—that aims to prohibit racialized law enforcement?

STATE AND FEDERAL LEGISLATION

States can uphold their own jurisdiction when it comes to *Whren*. For example, the New Jersey Supreme Court held that "objective" evidence that the police operated in a racially discriminatory manner will void any evidence seized in that instance in order to deter this form of policing.[28] Other states, such as Connecticut, North Carolina, Missouri, and Texas have established legislation mandating data collection on traffic stops, with several others recently introducing such legislation.[29]

One of the more stringent laws against racial profiling is the one passed by the Missouri State Assembly in 2000. There are three components of the Missouri law that makes it unique.[30] In direct contrast to *Whren*, pretextual stops are prohibited. Indeed, pretextual stop prevention must be implemented as policy, according to the text of the bill (Missouri General Assembly 2000):

> Each law enforcement agency shall adopt a policy on race-based traffic stops that: (1) Prohibits the practice of routinely stopping members of minority groups for violations of vehicle laws as a pretext for investigating other violations of criminal law; (2a) Determine whether any peace officers of the law enforcement agency have a pattern of stopping members of minority groups for violations of vehicle laws in a number disproportionate to the population of minority groups living within the jurisdiction of the law enforcement agency; (2b) If the review reveals a pattern, require an investigation to determine whether any peace officers of the law enforcement agency routinely stop members of minority groups for violations of vehicle laws as a pretext for investigating other violations of criminal law.

Unlike the *Whren* decision that effectively discounted the racial realities of profiling on our nation's roads, the language in the Missouri bill directly addresses the potential of law enforcement actions to be motivated by factors unrelated to the actual traffic violation that led to the stop. As such, the Missouri law contextualizes law enforcement powers within the racial order of society.

With the number of states adopting pretextual stop legislation on the rise, is the *Whren* decision still injurious? A decision by the U.S. Supreme Court that clearly recognizes the role of race in the police–minority relationship would serve as a message to law enforcement at large that things will not continue as business as usual. A federal law, however, is not without its drawbacks. Given the range of state laws adopted to collect information on racial profiling and to prohibit pretextual stops, there is the chance that some of the more stringent laws will be found in the state realm. Federal law may preempt local and state law that is somehow contradictory to it.[31]

Indeed, there is a history of legislative efforts to address racial profiling. The federal government has made some effort to legislate the documentation of racial profiling on a national level, following the lead taken by some state governments (the events of September 11, 2001, however, have complicated these efforts). Shortly before leaving office, President Clinton directed federal law enforcement to collect and report information on traffic stops.[32] After many attempts beginning in the late 1990s,

Representative John Conyers (D-MI) and Senator Russ Feingold (D-WI) recently introduced what is now referred to as the End Racial Profiling Act of 2004 to force local law enforcement agencies to uniformly collect data on the particulars of each traffic stop.[33] With the Obama presidency, there is formal discourse from his administration about a federal law against racial profiling.

There is little research on what the actual police experience is with racial profiling in regards to the social processes that facilitate its occurrence. No doubt the impact of residential segregation and spatial regulation figures prominently in the process, as do the associations with minority status and space with criminality. For example, consider the following quote from an earlier research project of mine.[34] When I asked a patrol sergeant to what extent he believed racial profiling occurred in law enforcement, he responded:

> if you want to talk about the public's view of racial profiling, which is, you see ah, you're in a predominantly minority neighborhood and somebody white driving through there at two o'clock in the morning looking for dope . . . or looking for a prostitute. You get behind them and stop them for a busted taillight. Well, you looked at them because it's the only car that's not, eh, that's not supposed to be in your area. You know that area, you know it well. You know everybody that lives around there. You see this car that's not supposed to be there at two o'clock in the morning. It catches your eye. You turn around on it. It's got a taillight. You knock it down. The public sees that as racial profiling. And I don't see that. Now does that happen? All the time. But does an officer stop just based on what they look like? I, I haven't seen it and I haven't done it.

The regulation of social space features prominently, with the minority status of the space in question regarded as off limits to the white motorist who *must* be in the minority space for criminal pursuit (because of the racial separation in our society, there is no consideration that a white motorist is a friend, coworker, lover of the area's residents). The officer is in fact describing a pretextual stop. In a racially ordered society such as the United States, the regulation of space by law enforcement matters. As suggested in an analysis of *United States v. Bell*, a selective enforcement case brought before the U.S. Supreme Court following the *Whren* decision:[35]

> The fact that police had adopted a zero-tolerance approach to traffic violations in this predominantly minority neighborhood explained the beyond-disparate arrest numbers. The implication is a dangerous one: Police may pursue distinctly different objectives in areas of differing concern through inconsistent enforcement of the same traffic code, even when those areas are primarily minority populated. Such a suggestion sounds remarkably like a

> judicial authorization of de facto discriminatory policing, a serious failure by a judiciary charged with protecting the constitutional rights of all citizens, black or white.

Laws proposed in an attempt to remedy the situation may suffer from noncompliance. Though somewhat anecdotal, during a research project I was doing on the police, the department I studied was also conducting its own internal research on racial profiling. Each officer was provided with scantronlike cards on which they were to mark the demographics of each driver they stopped, whether or not a citation was issued. Even with me in the patrol car with them, and with them knowing that I was doing research on police–minority relations, the majority of officers did not fill out the scantrons after each stop. As a researcher, I wondered why they were seemingly unconcerned with the consequences of not following the data collection procedures. Surely a system might have been in place to match the scantron reports with each radio interaction they had with dispatch indicating a stop was about to occur. This provides a micro-level example of noncompliance concerns with any affirmative race law if those charged with enforcing it disagree fundamentally with its premise and goal.

CONCLUSION

The 1996 *Whren* decision was a defining moment in the history of state protection of people of color in the United States. Virtually ignoring the racial realities of the twenty-first century, the justices considered a case that was essentially about race and the racial structure of our land and decided not only to not give the case a thorough review of the racial matters at its core, but to increase the law enforcement powers that were an inherent part of the problem being brought to their attention. Earlier standards of "probable cause" and "reasonable suspicion" from the *Terry v. Ohio* case gave way to affirmation of the pretextual stop. As noted in the sergeant's comments, these stops happen "all of the time." The weight of the ramifications from *Whren* on minority communities is heavy, with the legitimized authority of the state facilitating the maintenance of the racial order in the United States.

The *Whren* decision is a useful legal construct to examine racial profiling because it touches not only on the practice of racialized policing, but also on the discourse of racialized law in the United States. Given that all markers of social well-being are racially ordered in the United States, that sociological/criminological knowledge of communities of color perspectives of the state (via law enforcement, etc.) greatly differs from those of white America because of experiential realities between the two groups, the justices on the highest court in the land ushered in a monumental decision for the twenty-first century with *Whren*. Law enforcement officers who do not have *probable cause* or who cannot *articulate reasonable suspicion* now have legal cover to intervene on behalf of the (racial) state. The decision supports communities of color who have long held that racialized enforcement of the law is part of the experience of "being black" (or Latino).

The *Whren* decision, with its virtual avoidance of any discussion of race, reflects the current practice in the literature on racial profiling by mainstream criminology. All of this fits with the dominant racial ideology of the post-Civil Rights era, color-blind racism. The *Whren* decision is one component of how racialization processes operate in the contemporary era in formal realms. In chapter 3, I turn to an examination of what I argue is another manifestation of racialization, that of the formal realm of the academy and the mainstream approach of criminology in examining racial profiling.

NOTES

1. *Whren v. United States*. 1996. No. 95-5841. Supreme Court of the United States. Retrieved December 12, 2004. http://web.lexis-nexis.com/universe/printdoc.
2. Bonilla-Silva, Eduardo. 2003. *Racism without Racists: Color-Blind Racism and the Persistence of Racial Inequality in the United States*. Lanham, MD: Rowman & Littlefield.
3. Harris, David A. 1997. "'Driving While Black' and All Other Traffic Offenses: The Supreme Court and Pretextual Traffic Stops." *Journal of Criminal Law and Criminology* 87: 544–82, p. 549.
4. *Whren v. United States*, p. 3.
5. Harris, "'Driving While Black' and All Other Traffic Offenses," p. 7.
6. Hall, John C. 1996. "Pretext Traffic Stops: *Whren v. United States*." Retrieved December 6, 2004, p. 5. www.fbi.gov/publications/leb/1996/nov965.txt.
7. Bonilla-Silva, *Racism without Racists*.
8. Hall, John C. 1996. "Pretext Traffic Stops," p. 6.
9. Crawford, Kimberly A. 1995. "Pretext Seizures." *FBI Law Enforcement Bulletin*. 64: 28–33, p. 28.
10. Buerger, Michael, and Amy Farrell. 2002. "The Evidence of Racial Profiling: Differing Interpretations of Documented and Unofficial Sources." *Police Quarterly* 5: 272–305, p. 274.
11. Milazzo, Carl, and Ron Hansen. 1999 (Nov.). "Race Relations in Police Operations: A Legal and Ethical Perspective." Paper presented at the 106th annual conference of the International Association of Chiefs of Police, Charlotte, NC.
12. United Nations Committee on the Elimination of Racial Discrimination. 2001 (Aug. 6, Geneva). Reply from U.S. Assistant Attorney General Ralph F. Boyd, Jr., and U.S. Assistant Secretary of State Lorne Craner. Retrieved December 6, 2004, p. 3. www.usdoj.gov/crt/speeches/boydgenevaqanda.htm.

13. Harris, "'Driving While Black' and All Other Traffic Offenses."

14. Davis, Angela J. 1997. "Race, Cops, and Traffic Stops." *University of Miami Law Review* 51: 6.

15. Cooper, Christopher. 2003. "Unlawful Motives and Race-Based Arrest for Minor Offenses." *Justice Policy Journal* 1: 3–17.

16. Cooper, "Unlawful Motives and Race-Based Arrest for Minor Offenses," p. 3.

17. Milazzo and Hansen, "Race Relations in Police Operations: A Legal and Ethical Perspective."

18. Milazzo and Hansen, "Race Relations in Police Operations: A Legal and Ethical Perspective," p. 4.

19. Harris, "'Driving While Black' and All Other Traffic Offenses," p. 546.

20. Davis, "Race, Cops, and Traffic Stops," p. 2.

21. *Whren v. United States*, p. 8.

22. Bonilla-Silva, *Racism without Racists*.

23. Russell, Katheryn K. 1998. *The Color of Crime: Racial Hoaxes, White Fear, Black Protectionism, Police Harassment, and Other Macroaggressions*. New York: New York University Press, p. 134.

24. Davis, Peggy C. 2000 [1989]. "Law as Microaggression." Pp. 141–51 in *Critical Race Theory: The Cutting Edge,* Richard Delgado and Jean Stefancic, eds. Philadelphia, PA: Temple University Press, p. 149.

25. *Whren v. United States*, p. 10.

26. Milazzo and Hansen, "Race Relations in Police Operations: A Legal and Ethical Perspective," p. 3.

27. Russell, *The Color of Crime*, p. 131.

28. Cooper, "Unlawful Motives and Race-Based Arrest for Minor Offenses," p. 9.

29. Ward, James D. 2002. "Race, Ethnicity, and Law Enforcement Profiling: Implications for Public Policy." *Public Administration Review* 62: 726–35.

30. Ward, "Race, Ethnicity, and Law Enforcement Profiling."

31. Ward, "Race, Ethnicity, and Law Enforcement Profiling."

32. Meeks, Kenneth. 2000. *Driving While Black: Highways, Shopping Malls, Taxicabs, Sidewalks: How to Fight Back If You Are a Victim of Racial Profiling*. New York: Broadway Books.

33. Feingold, Russ. 2004. "Feingold Introduces the End Racial Profiling Act of 2004." February 26, 2004. Press release. Retrieved December 14, 2004. http://feingold.senate.gov/releases/04/02/2004304407.html.

34. Glover, Karen S. 2007. "Police Discourse on Racial Profiling." *Journal of Contemporary Criminal Justice* 23: 239–47.

35. Hall, Christopher. 1998. "Challenging Selective Enforcement of Traffic Regulations after the Disharmonic Convergence: *Whren v. United States, United States v. Armstrong*, and the Evolution of Police Discretion." *Texas Law Review* 76: 1083–123, p. 1108.

II

3

The Racial Project of Mainstream Criminology's Approach to Understanding Racial Profiling

> Racism is structural: a network of social relations at social, political, economic, and ideological levels that shapes the life chances of the various races . . . activists struggling against racial oppression and analysts wishing to understand how racial matters operate in any setting must have as their primary goal understanding a society's racial structure. This means that they must investigate the practices and mechanisms that produce and reproduce racial inequality in a society.
>
> (Eduardo Bonilla-Silva[1])

The purpose of this chapter is to forward our understanding of how the "practices and mechanisms" of racism—the brainchild of white logic—operate in racial profiling research. Racism is not about individual manifestations of animus but social arrangements (for example, practices and discourses) that shore up the social structure of the racial state. Mainstream criminology's effort to examine racial profiling has avoided serious engagement of race and racism in large part because of the methodology and theoretical approaches that dominate the discipline, even when race itself is a fundamental component of the studies.

To demonstrate the white logic orientation of current racial profiling research, I examine and critique in this chapter their guiding methodological and theoretical approaches. For example, one of the main topics of discussion in this chapter concerns the "perception"-oriented research in what I refer to as the second wave of racial profiling research. This area of inquiry by mainstream criminology researchers asks people of color what it was that made them *perceive* certain practices as racial domination, rather than ask, as a critical race orientation would direct, what those practices meant to them. From a critical race framework, the political context of "why do you see it that way?" is problematic, while the "what does it mean to you?" alternative provides politically silenced voices access to contextualize the experience. Because of the predominating view, although racial profiling operates as entree into the criminal justice system for communities of color and thus influences *life chances*, virtually no substantive data exist on what the experience means to communities of color as a function of racial oppression. I expand on these concerns further in this chapter.

Covington describes how long-term claims by people of color of being targeted by the police were often viewed as anecdotal accounts from overly sensitive, angry, and disgruntled people of color.[2] While racial minorities have voiced resistance to racializing and criminalizing processes for centuries, the body of research now available on racial profiling specifically was established only in the past decade. This is an example of how white-dominated social science—criminology being one of the more influential disciplines in the past century—neglected to document issues illuminating racial oppression and its dynamics. Bonilla-Silva argues that social control of communities of color (that includes the production of knowledge about racial ordering processes) are in effect rendered invisible to large numbers of Americans:[3]

> They are rendered invisible in four ways. First, because the enforcement of the racial order from the 1960s onward has been institutionalized, individual whites can express a detachment from the racialized ways in which social control agencies operate in the United States. Second, because these agencies are legally charged with maintaining order in society, their actions are deemed neutral and necessary. Thus, it is no surprise that whereas blacks mistrust the police in surveys, whites consistently support them. Third, journalists and academicians investigating crime are central agents in the reproduction of distorted views on crime. . . . Finally, incidents that seem to indicate racial bias in the criminal justice system are depicted by white-dominated media as isolated incidents.

An examination of the current literature on racial profiling demonstrates many of these concerns. My examination of the racial profiling literature specifically revealed that (1) the focus is on the micro-level and the individual police–minority encounter; (2) it is almost exclusively quantitative; (3) it is lacking a theoretical context, particularly a race theory context; and (4) there exists a *rearticulation* of the direction of racial profiling research characteristic of a *racial project*.[4] As well, these limitations intersect.

FIRST WAVE OF RACIAL PROFILING RESEARCH

For analytical purposes, I distinguish two waves of research on racial profiling. I first engage a number of the characteristics of the current body of literature on racial profiling from a critical race methodological eye. As noted above, the traits of racial profiling research as it is currently embodied are intertwined and my analysis here reflects that interrelation.

With rare exceptions, racial profiling research examines the relationship between communities of color and law enforcement as one bounded by individual-level interactions. For instance, research inquiries focus on law enforcement officer attributes, suspect demeanor, and how these characteristics might influence the particular traffic stop under examination—that is, what is it about the officer that influences the encounter and what is it about the citizen that influences the encounter. Similarly, the bulk of data available on the police–minority relationship primarily address civilian attitudes toward the police.[5] These studies show a racial differential in attitudes toward the police, with people of color expressing less support for the police than whites. The survey approach, a quantitative method, is limited in what it can reveal about the larger context of the degree of support. Emphasis on the individual tends to discount the larger structural forces that influence the social world.

As evident in the public discourse following a high-profile incident of police abuse of force (for example, the state violence directed at Rodney King, Amadou Diallo, and Sean Bell), racial profiling concerns voiced by people of color emerge as a key factor in explaining the disparity in attitudes toward support for the police. This public discourse often provides insight into the broader sociolegal realm of citizenship that people of color are actually addressing when they indicate low levels of support for law enforcement. Without the context of the state violence incidents to situate these attitudes, the lower levels of support for law enforcement by communities of color (always in comparison to the standard of whiteness) may be exploited discursively to posit people of color as *anti-law and order*. On the contrary, people of color are frequently the staunchest defenders of the rights, duties, and protections accorded United States citizens under the law.[6]

The individual-level orientation is demonstrated by a recent piece in *Criminology*, the most revered journal in mainstream criminology (and almost exclusively quantitative in nature). A good example of the narrow context racial profiling processes are examined in is evident in the authors' comment that racial profiling "has been blamed for a variety of ills, from increasing friction between the police and minority communities to overall decreased confidence in and cooperation with the police."[7] The recent piece "'Police Don't Like Black People': African-American

Young Men's Accumulated Police Experiences" is one of the few qualitative examinations of racial profiling in recent literature and extends our understanding of young black males' encounters with the police through the narrative, particularly the cumulative effects of race-based policing on attitudes toward the police.[8] It is useful as one of the growing calls for more qualitative work on the policing of communities of color. However, the author's examination is oriented to the encounter itself, like the majority of racial profiling scholarship, and thus misses the larger ramifications of racialization and criminalization processes by the state and the broader realm of citizenship that this book ultimately reveals.

The concept of micro- and macro-aggressions may be useful here.[9] Micro-aggressions are discriminatory and racializing actions from dominant group members against subordinate group members in one-on-one encounters. A racializing and criminalizing comment from a law enforcement officer to a citizen provides an example. In contrast, macro-aggressions are racializing actions and discourses that negatively affect whole groups. An example here would be the constant media portrayals of young men of color as criminals and people to be feared. While one image on the evening news does represent criminalization of that particular individual, the *criminalblackman* stereotype[10] so prominent in the white mind ensures that the imagery is disbursed to any young male of color, thus its macro-level aggression effect. Both micro- and macro-aggressions have negative effects on society. Racial profiling engages these harmful effects on both levels. The individual officer engaging in micro-aggressions reinforces the historical and contemporary macro-aggression inherent to policing of communities of color.

In addition to focusing on the bounded relationship of the law enforcement officer and the individual motorist—which I argue distances more structural influences of racism from the analysis—what I refer to as the first wave of racial profiling research is almost exclusively quantitative. The focus is disproportionality in law enforcement-initiated traffic stops. Namely, the main inquiry of the first wave of research is, Are motorists of color subject to traffic stops (considered seizures under Fourth Amendment protections against *unreasonable searches and seizures* by the state) *disproportionate* to their representation in the general driving population? These studies demonstrate racial disparity in traffic stops, with more minority motorists relative to white motorists being stopped by law enforcement.[11] The first wave of research on racial profiling also included quantitative studies on key factors in police decision-making processes, suspect demeanor, and officer attributes.[12]

There is little theoretical grounding with the first wave of these studies, even as noted by leading scholars themselves.[13] This reflects the general atheoretical orientation in criminology as a discipline. In those instances where a theoretical push is made to contextualize racial profiling, it typically emerges from a basic conflict theory framework. For example, in a recent study researchers briefly discuss conflict theory and how the law is differentially enforced against racial minorities in society to protect white interests.[14] Other research looks at Herbert Blumer's group-position theory, to describe how dominant groups view the police as allies.[15] Some researchers have discussed how cognitive bias and its associated concept of in-group bias explains the disproportionate numbers of motorists of color stopped by the police.[16] Racial prejudice, though rarely directly discussed at length (and not necessarily subsumed under the above-mentioned concepts), is another factor in examinations of racial profiling motivations.[17] The prejudice concern of Wilson et al.'s study is very much grounded in the traditional view of how race operates in society—racism is basically negative attitudes about other racial groups forwarded by individuals who merely need to be educated or removed from society in order to bring about racial equality. The solution is simple: Get rid of the racists and racism will abate. More critical analysis finds that the prejudice focus of this type of approach does not expose the dominant form of racism—color-blind racism—that has emerged in the post-Civil Rights era.[18] Spatial context is also looked to in explaining racial disparities in policing behavior.[19]

Racial profiling is frequently framed in the context of an economics-based argument known as *statistical* or *rational discrimination* theory.[20] Rational discrimination arguments point to the preponderance of minorities in the criminal justice system to justify targeted law enforcement actions. Variations of this white logic approach to explaining the racial disparity in traffic stops appear regularly in both academic and public domain discourses on racial profiling, remaining a virulent argument to counter contestation of racialized policing. The thrust of the argument is commonsensical, thus explaining its draw for public consumption: People of color are disproportionately stopped compared to whites because they are disproportionately involved in criminal activity.[21] The obvious tautology of the argument, however, is rarely engaged—the criminal justice system looks the way it does because of racialized law enforcement. Russell[22] offers another complication of the simplistic position of the rational discrimination argument in the following:

> Many people would argue that it is unfair to blame the police for being suspicious of Black men. After all, Black men are disproportionately engaged in crime. It is reasonable, then, that the police disproportionately suspect them of criminal activity. Black men do commit street crimes at high rates—rates far exceeding their percentage in the U.S. population (6 percent). The important question, however, is, "Are Black men stopped and questioned by the police at a rate that greatly exceeds their rate of street crime?" If so, the high

> number of police stops cannot be legally justified . . . the available research suggests that Black men are stopped and questioned at a rate much higher than the level of their involvement in crime.

It is important to highlight the distinction that black men (men of color more generally) commit more street crime, rather than what is known as "white-collar crime" (generally that crime committed in the corporate world, industry, government, etc.). The social harm arising from white-collar crime (monetary loss, bodily injury, and death) is far greater than that arising from street crime in any given year.[23] Of course, the media attention directed to street crime overwhelms that given to white-collar crime, even given the social harm created by the latter. This white-framed media attention helps shape public policy from local to federal levels and redirects attention from the massive social harms produced by white-collar crime. The location of white-collar crime in the "suites, not the streets"—also shapes the deployment of law enforcement resources and thus serves as one of the arguments sometimes given in the disproportionality-oriented studies that high crime areas (always a referent to street crime) demand that more law enforcement agents are deployed to those areas.

Another flaw representative of the white logic orientation of this part of the research is the contradiction found in the literature's emphasis on *rationality* when one of the main theories engaged from a race perspective in that same literature is one based on *irrationality*. That is, the rational discrimination argument is fundamentally about using the official rates of offending (based on already-flawed arrest rates or incarceration rates, for instance) by racial groups to justify targeted law enforcement attention to racial minority groups. Yet, the main race theory engaged by mainstream racial profiling researchers views racism as an *irrational* response by individually prejudiced social actors whose reeducation, reform, or removal from society, will bring on the end of racism. For instance, removing the irrational or sick individual police officer from the ranks will lead to less racialized policing in that department.

In sum, the first wave of racial profiling research is almost exclusively quantitative and largely void of theoretical guidance. It primarily sought to document the practice of the traffic stop to determine if there was disproportionality in stops across racial groups. A general consensus followed from increasingly sophisticated studies to support longtime claims from communities of color that they were targeted for police attention based on nonbehavioral characteristics. While it is outside of the domain of this book, it is important to state that studies to address the issue of "hit rates"—the rates of contraband found, such as illegal weapons and drugs—indicate that people of color do not have higher hit rates than whites.[24] The premise of the rational discrimination argument is thus given a serious blow. Indeed, some studies show that whites have higher hit rates than people of color, an idea theorized in Bernard Hartcourt's book *Against Prediction: Profiling, Policing, and Punishing in an Actuarial Age*[25] in which he presents a compelling argument that racial profiling processes lead to more crime in society because whites understand they are not under the panopticon of the state and thus operate under the premise that they can commit crime and go undetected. Yet on the heels of all of the data indicating racialized law enforcement is a mainstay of the racial minority experience, the research agenda took an interesting turn that is the subject of the next section on the second wave of racial profiling research from mainstream criminology.

TREND TO PERCEPTION-BASED RESEARCH

Racial profiling research was firmly at the top of the mainstream criminological agenda in the 1990s and early 2000s. As the body of literature grew, it focused on developing more accurate methodology to get at the issue of disproportionality evident in the numerous studies that were now available.

On the heels of the plethora of data documenting racial disparity in traffic stops, an interesting turn occurred in the focus of racial profiling research—a trend to perception-based research. The empirical focus on racial disparity in traffic stops was followed by more quantitative studies in this second wave of research exploring factors influencing an individual's "perception" of being racially profiled.[26] As briefly discussed earlier, perception-oriented research is concerned with what makes someone perceive they have been racially profiled or suffered discriminatory treatment by law enforcement.

As a critical race framework directs, this turn in the research needs to be examined politically. Omi and Winant's notion of *rearticulation* as well as their *racial project* concept are appropriate theoretical constructs to engage from a critical perspective.[27] Rearticulation refers to both overt and covert efforts by the state and other dominating social institutions to shift, absorb, and/or refigure a given social issue. Hence, the move in the racial profiling literature to one concerned with perceptions may reflect a desire to *rearticulate* racial profiling within the academy, or within public policy, or indeed among the arbiters of cultural commentary. This may be partially explained by the sometimes symbiotic relationship those studying the police have with the police, as well as with the general demographic profile of researchers and criminologists of police studies more generally. The *racial project* is a mechanism that facilitates, reconfigures, and portrays racial dynamics in order to claim and redistribute resources and control; it may also explain the dramatic switch in focus of racial profiling research.[28] The racial project, as used here, operates as a mechanism to explain or interpret racial dynamics that ultimately maintains the racial status quo. I contend that this perplexing turn to issues of perception in the racial profiling research deflects attention from law enforcement (in the current analysis, the racial state) and shifts the emphasis to the citizen.

It is interesting to note that the perception-oriented research goes against mainstream criminology's traditional claim that researchers, and no one else for that matter, are able to get into the mind of law enforcement to know what motivating factors—racial or otherwise—facilitated potentially unfair treatment of the citizenry. Claims of racialized policing were summarily dismissed and viewed as individual-level processes unable to be answered because they were locked up in the minds of individual law enforcement agents. Yet, the second wave of racial profiling research topping the research agenda currently asks the recipients of racialized law enforcement to expound upon why they *perceive* they have been racially profiled. There is not a similar framing of this inquiry as has traditionally been the case when attempting to understand law enforcement "perceptions" of criminality in those receiving law enforcement attention. The doubt expressed earlier with this inquiry into the mind seems to have been dispelled when the subjects under study are those making claims against the racial state. Traditional criminologists now consider this a valid research approach. Clearly, both inquiries go to the mind of the respondent—whether the officer or the motorist—though in different contexts.

It is clear that the perception-oriented research, as it is currently discussed in the racial profiling literature, suggests an *in your head* perspective to understanding racial profiling experiences. This is evident in the recurring theme in the current literature to distinguish "perceptions" from "reality." From a critical race perspective, this perspective invalidates claims of racial profiling made by communities of color when it is successful in framing the experience as a matter of *perception* and not necessarily *reality*.

For example, leading scholars state the following: "Citizens' *perceptions* of police stops may be considered just as important as the objective *reality* of such stops" (italics mine).[29] In this case, the authors—leading scholars in the racial profiling literature realm—not only make a distinction between perception and reality, but, also, by stating that the reality is "objective," create a greater cleavage between the citizen experience (the "perception") and what is considered to be the "objective" truth. Ironically, the objective truth's source is an ultimately *subjective* assessment of the traffic stop *by law enforcement*. In another instance, the same authors contrast "perceived threats" with "not necessarily real threats."[30] Later in their piece, after laying out an extensive analysis about the effects of racial and ethnic status on policing, the authors state: "Of course, *perceived* experience with police bias is not necessarily equivalent to *actual* discrimination. . . ."[31] This idea is echoed in another recent study in which a noted scholar states that "perceptions" of racial profiling and injustice may not reflect the "*actual*" policing practices.[32]

Leading researchers Ronald Weitzer and Steven A. Tuch identify a key point that illustrates the white logic of the social sciences when the authors briefly discuss the gap between people of color and whites when it comes to believing the police treat these groups differently. The "overwhelming majority" of whites (+75 percent) believed that blacks and Latinos have experiences *similar* to whites when encountering the police.[33] According to the authors, this is in line with research on racial discrimination in other aspects of society where whites generally see it as "isolated and episodic" instead of fundamental to social processes in the United States. This tendency helps explain the orientation in mainstream criminology to not address racial profiling as a manifestation of larger racial contexts that shape everyday life for communities of color. It also gives context for the tendency of mainstream criminology racial profiling researchers to devalue people of color by not engaging—to any serious degree—their politically silenced voices. The notion that whites can suggest discrimination is "isolated" behavior in the face of the racialized social order in the United States and is testament to the power of white supremacy.

Another example of the discursive maneuvers mainstream criminology engages comes in an examination of attributions the public makes about legal officials who engage in behavior such as racial profiling. As is the case with much of the discourse in racial profiling studies to date, the authors clearly make a distinction between what they refer to as "objective" and "subjective" realities of racial profiling: "our analysis focuses on the *subjective* experience of feeling profiled rather than the *objective* one of being profiled. We do this because we believe that the experience of receiving police attention based on one's race—regardless of whether profiling has occurred—may be responsible for many of the negative associations of racial profiling."[34]

Many of the studies on racial profiling, particularly those addressing issues of perception, include some reference to the objective–subjective dichotomy. From a critical perspective, this has the effect of diminishing accounts of racial profiling by communities of color. Interestingly, textbook definitions of *perception* include descriptors such as distinguish, observe, awareness, and sense; they do not present the term as a contrast to reality. The current literature's emphasis on perception discursively signals distance from reality in accessing racial minority views on the criminal justice system. As such, this discursive orientation of the mainstream research operates in the white logic framework forwarded by Zuberi and Bonilla-Silva.[35]

With that stated, because I take as my premise the understanding that racial profiling occurs with some regularity in communities of color, the issue of perception becomes irrelevant in the data analysis to follow. Manifestations of racial oppression such as racial profiling are routine activities of the larger social condition and emerge from the "organized set" of racialized ideas and acts comprising the white racial frame.[36] My interest is not to determine if racial profiling occurs objectively, as the numerous studies on the actual practice of race-based policing have already demonstrated this to be the case. Nor is my interest to determine why people of color "perceive" racial profiling—the subjective issue. I am concerned with the effects of racial profiling on those who experience it—the broader contexts that frame the experience for people of color and the larger meanings they associate with the practice.

THEORY IN PERCEPTION RESEARCH

Theory about what factors shape citizens' perceptions of racial profiling focus on citizens' "personal and vicarious" experiences.[37] In the mainstream literature, personal experiences include research participants' own accounts of being stopped by law enforcement, while vicarious experiences involve research participants' sense of imagined participation from family, friends, and others' accounts, including media. By focusing on the personal experience of those who have perceived racial profiling, again, the approach of racial profiling researchers is on the individual level. To provide a counterapproach to understanding the perception issue, in chapters 6 and 7, I provide a qualitative examination of personal and vicarious issues as experienced by people of color in their encounters with the racial state. As the interviews in the two data chapters demonstrate, a personal encounter with law enforcement goes well beyond the bounded relationship that is the subject of mainstream racial profiling research. The present examination of vicarious experience (discussed in chapter 7) is also informative in understanding the traditional criminology approach to racial profiling as its underlying subtext is that communities of color may distort and exaggerate racial experience. Analyses of white discourse on racism frequently show whites dismissing, discounting, and justifying "complaints" from people of color about the everydayness of racial oppression in contemporary America.[38]

RACE THEORY IN THE PERCEPTION-ORIENTED LITERATURE

In the rare instances when it does engage race theory, the perception-oriented research uses classic race theory frameworks, limitations that I briefly addressed earlier when contextualized within the new form of racism in the contemporary era. In a recent book by leading police studies scholars Weitzer and Tuch, *Race and Policing in America: Conflict and Reform* (2006), the authors themselves critique the current state of racial profiling research for its lack of a theoretical base. To this end, the authors engage a classic race theory—Blumer's group-position thesis—in an attempt to situate racial profiling processes into a theoretical context. The group-position thesis concerns racial and ethnic group competition for valued resources, among other issues. The authors extend Blumer's original work to include "groups' relations with social institutions" to explain why the criminal justice system at large may be viewed with "affinity" by dominant group members.[39] Consequently, the theory helps explain the differential in attitudes toward the police among racial groups.

Their goal to introduce race theory into the literature is useful. The authors conclude that "*Race matters* a great deal."[40] However, we are still far from understanding the significance of racialization and criminalization processes expressed via the traffic stop. Although *Race and Policing in America* includes a modicum of qualitative data (that they describe as able to provide a "more nuanced" and "deeper understanding" of how people experience policing),[41] its survey orientation and engagement of group position theory[42] is limited in offering an understanding of the context and meanings of racialization and criminalization processes by the state.

The dated nature of the group-position theory is worth commenting on briefly. I note, however, that Blumer's work is highly regarded as one of the earlier race theories that did attempt to direct attention away from the *prejudiced individual* orientation of race theory. Originating in the 1950s, the theory was directed at a distinctly *different* formation of racism than what generally manifests in the contemporary era.[43] The overt displays of racial dominance by whites in earlier eras, particularly in police practices to uphold racist laws, are now subsumed under less obvious practices such as racial profiling. Part of what critical approaches—whether concerning race, class, gender, or sexuality—intend to do is uncover the myriad forms of oppression that are (more or less) cloaked in normalized, hegemonic operations of the state. Thus, I argue, a critical race approach is more appropriate to understanding the manifestations of racism in the post-Civil Rights era. A premise of this book is that racial profiling processes—though wholly evident as racialized events to social actors who experience the phenomenon—are regularly rationalized, justified, and neutralized by mainstream criminology and, as a result, (academically) diminished as a social force that helps reproduce the racial order. Like other critical-oriented engagements of established knowledge, critical race theory is concerned with exposing the dominant discourses that nurture white supremacy ideology as it retools racial practices in the contemporary era. In this instance, for example, my focus on deconstructing the perception discourse found in the current literature on racial profiling meets this goal of critical theory.

RACISM AS PREJUDICE

Another example of the limits of theoretical engagement of the race realm comes from leading police studies researchers in a 2004 piece *Prejudice in Police Profiling: Assessing an Overlooked Aspect in Prior Research.*[44] The authors' emphasis on racial *prejudice* points to a micro-level perspective of how racial minority status operates in society, one that is bounded in a belief and attitude system. They provide a lengthy review of classic race literature on stereotyping, attribution bias, and the like, all of which are mainstays of social psychological thought. The authors acknowledge that few studies directly address the racial component of racial profiling but the authors still fail to view the possibilities in this regard beyond racial animus or racial prejudice frameworks. More critical race analyses recognize the importance of ideology and attitudes with racism, but consider broader social structures, including the intersectionality of class, gender, and sexuality concerns with race as more fundamental to the reproduction of oppression in contemporary times. The racialized traffic stop is a mere manifestation of broader, racist social forces underpinning American political and legal realms.[45] Bonilla-Silva argues that "although 'racism' has a definite ideological component, reducing racial phenomenon to ideas limits the possibility of how it shapes race's life chances" and is thus "ultimately viewed as a psychological phenomenon to be examined at the individual level."[46] In examinations of racial profiling that focus on the individual *prejudiced* motivations of the police officer, the suggestion is that, if the deviant officer is removed, the racial problem is removed. Critical examinations consider racism as structural and systemic, a much more expansive conception than prejudice-oriented frameworks suggest.[47]

As demonstrated by many of the mainstream studies on police–minority relations, racial status is a determinant factor in attitudes toward the police. Zuberi argues that the "race effect" is a more accurate understanding of how scientists should portray race in their analyses, particularly when race is not clearly contextualized as a social construction in analyses.[48] Race as a social construction has generated the inequalities that allow "race" to take on a life of its own in the social sciences.[49] Finally, some theorize that the overall experience of racial oppression with other social institutions operates as a "priming" mechanism for communities of color in shaping perceptions of police behavior.[50]

IT'S NOT RACE, IT'S CLASS

Examinations of race matters frequently look to socioeconomic status to explain the racial order in the United States. This classic "it's not race, it's class" debate is a centerpiece of white logic in the social sciences. One early study in the racial profiling literature examined the influence of race, class, and perceived personal experience with racial profiling and how they shape attitudes toward the police.[51] Part of the discussion centers on whether higher levels of socioeconomic status may insulate people of color from unfair police treatment and other social disadvantage, suggested in William Julius Wilson's[52] declining significance of race thesis, or whether higher class attainment does not necessarily operate as a preventative status for communities of color[53] because racial profiling enables someone to be "stripped of status at a moment's notice. . . ."[54]

The authors' examination of the literature suggests that there are mixed results from previous studies that have specifically looked at the effects of socioeconomic status on attitudes toward the police. One dramatic finding from the 1999 study is that while nearly three out of four young black males believe they have experienced racial profiling, only about one in ten young, white males thought they have been stopped by the police because of racial or ethnic status. This result in and of itself suggests the need for qualitative work for insight into this great disparity.

PROCEDURAL JUSTICE FRAMEWORK

One of the more critical theoretical engagements in the mainstream research to predict perceptions of racial profiling is the concept of procedural fairness. The three components of procedural justice are (1) quality of decision making—perceived neutrality and consistency; (2) quality of treatment—being treated with dignity and respect, having one's rights acknowledged; and (3) trustworthiness—believing that the authorities are acting out of benevolence and a sincere desire to be fair."[55] Primary researchers in this area, looking at four sets of data they collected on various aspects of policing, conclude that when individuals are treated politely and respectfully and have their rights acknowledged, they are less likely to experience a traffic stop as race based. A similar concept to procedural justice is *distributive justice*, where the fairness of the outcome (is justice, punishment, etc., equally distributed?) of a given citizen–police encounter is determinant in how one experiences the encounter. As discussed in chapter 5 on citizenship, these two concepts are related to the broader concept of citizenship as there is a focus on equal treatment under the law. However, procedural justice, as it is engaged in the current literature, does not illuminate how the disparate treatment impacts the lives of those social actors affected by it.

Another study that engages the procedural justice and distributive justice concepts includes a lengthy review of several studies on attitudes toward the police and the racial differential that generally emerges in these studies.[56] While useful to some extent, this examination clearly demonstrates that the bulk of research on police–minority relations is survey based and thus limited in contextualization of the procedural and distributive justice ideals it theoretically posits as explanatory. The author herself acknowledges the limitation in the reviewed studies in the following excerpt: "Unfortunately, the research reviewed above has been unable to examine the specific circumstances of citizens' experiences and how these factors shape citizens' perceptions of justice and injustice." Yet, after acknowledging this limitation in the mainstream approach to racial profiling, the author relies on another survey-based data set (the 1999 Police-Public Contact Survey) in her attempt to extend our understandings of the issue. The author concludes that citizens' perceptions of injustice with law enforcement, including racial profiling processes, are influenced by "the perceived *fairness* of the procedures and outcomes they receive."[57] Interestingly, the procedural fairness framework described above is critiqued in recent research[58] that links *perceptions* of unfair sanctions (e.g., racial profiling) to individual low *self-control* issues traditionally considered criminogenic in themselves.

Perception-oriented research clearly focuses on the individual and the psychological. Research that treats racial matters in the context of mere perceptions or ideas distances structural elements of racial oppression. Examining racial matters as merely ideas "limits the possibility of understanding how it [race] shapes . . . life chances."[59] Brilliantly described by Derrick Bell, racial matters operate "in the real lives of black and white people, not in sentimental caverns of the mind."[60]

THE QUANTITATIVE TREND CONTINUES—PERCEPTION DATA

Given this orientation toward ideas in a fairly consuming research agenda examining perceptions, the perception research is unexpectedly based almost exclusively on quantitative analysis. For example, a survey-based study attempting to explain Latino perceptions of racial profiling included the following questions: (1) Have you had a good experience with the police? (2) Have you had a bad experience with the police? (3) Have you ever been a victim of crime? (4) What is your political philosophy?[61] The respondent is limited in the quality of response they can provide for these inquiries. For example, a bad experience with the police could range from a simple speeding ticket to an incident with traumatizing use of force. In-depth understanding of the larger implications of racialized policing is limited given the quantitative approach dominating the current literature. Indeed, many recent criminology studies have called for further qualitative examination of racial differentials in law enforcement experiences.

The orientation of the literature is particularly troublesome when a number of the current studies claim that the citizens' experience is vital to understanding the phenomenon yet note that there has been scarce attention paid to how the public views the racialized traffic stop, "despite the fact that traffic stops are by far the most common site of police-citizen interaction."[62] Yet, the vast majority of studies do not engage in qualitative work to reveal the important meanings inherent to the phenomenon that only the narrative can provide. Leading researchers[63] in the field acknowledge that the perspective of the citizen is a crucial element to understanding racial profiling yet ultimately rely on quantitative survey data for illumination of the citizen view. Surveys limit the free flow of ideas and constrain the range of possible answers for respondents.[64] A 2005 study in the leading journal *Social Forces* is initially framed as a response to the *lack of research on* "citizens' views of and reported experiences with police bias," yet relies upon survey data to illuminate this void in the literature.[65] For example, the survey asks "Have you ever felt that you were stopped by the police just because of your race or ethnic background," and "Have you ever felt that you were treated unfairly by the police specifically because of your neighborhood?"

QUANTITATIVE VERSUS QUALITATIVE WORK

Qualitative work has been shown to offer a more consistent interpretation of social phenomenon than quantitative work alone, primarily as a result of respondents having the space and flexibility to contextualize answers to questions, in addition to allowing the researcher to probe participant responses for clarification, expansion, and meaning.[66] The "methodological individualism" that orients much survey research limits our ability to understand the vast and varied meanings that accompany race-related issues in contemporary times.[67] This is the case for both understanding whites' racial views and for understanding racial views of communities of color. For example, the data in the criminology literature on blacks' views of the police and racism in law enforcement are bounded by somewhat ambiguous—while simultaneously restrictive—inquiries about levels of support for the police. First, people of color indicate a strong sense of how the law—and therefore agents of the law—should operate in society. They are highly supportive of the ideals surrounding the law yet understand experientially that the practice of law and law enforcement in the United States is racialized. Second, inquiries about support for the police or particular experiences with the police point to the *individualism* traditionally (and contemporarily) associated with racism in the United States. By restricting the respondent to scales such as "agree" or "disagree" with *police* policies and philosophies, the associations to broader sociolegal realms made by communities of color when considering law enforcement are missed. As demonstrated by the data analysis in chapters 6 and 7, inquiries about the police, for many people of color, are not bounded to the individual officer who makes the traffic stop but to endemic racialized practices of domination by the larger entity of the state. Practices by the individual-level officer are "intrinsically connected to the field of racialized social relations" facilitated by the state.[68]

CONCLUSION

I have laid out a number of limitations with the current state of racial profiling research—its focus on the individual encounter and the citizen–officer dyad, its almost exclusive engagement of quantitative methods despite its own acknowledgment that better understandings of the citizen view is crucial, and its limited capacity to contextualize racial profiling in contemporary understandings of race theory. In the next chapter, I discuss my approach to understanding the racial profiling phenomenon through engagement of critical race methodology and theoretical frameworks that contextualize the phenomenon as one concerned with racial oppression.

NOTES

1. Bonilla-Silva, Eduardo. 2003. *Racism without Racists: Color-Blind Racism and the Persistence of Racial Inequality in the United States*. Lanham, MD: Rowman & Littlefield Publishers, pp. 90, 194.

2. Covington, Jeannette. 2001. "Round Up the Usual Suspects: Racial Profiling and the War on Drugs." Pp. 27–42 in *Petit Apartheid in the U.S. Criminal Justice System: The Dark Figure of Racism,* Dragan Milovanovic and Katheryn K. Russell, eds. Durham, NC: Carolina Academic Press.

3. Bonilla-Silva, *Racism without Racists,* p. 111.

4. Omi, Michael, and Howard Winant. 1994. *Racial Formation in the United States from the 1960s to the 1990s*. New York: Routledge.

5. Hagan, John, and Celesta Albonetti. 1982. "Race, Class, and the Perception of Criminal Injustice in America." *American Journal of Sociology* 88: 329–55; Parker, Keith D., Anne B. Onyekwuluje, and Komanduri S. Murty. 1995. "African-Americans' Attitudes toward the Police: A Multivariate Study." *Journal of Black Studies* 25: 396–409; Pate, Antony M., and Lorie A. Fridell. 1993. *Police Use of Force: Official Reports, Citizen Complaints, and Legal Consequences*. Washington, DC: Police Foundation; Tuch, Steven A., and Ronald Weitzer. 1997. "The Polls-Trends: Racial Differences in Attitudes toward the Police." *Public Opinion Quarterly* 61: 642–63; Weitzer, Ronald, and Steven A. Tuch. 2006. *Race and Policing in America: Conflict and Reform*. Cambridge, UK: Cambridge University Press.

6. Feagin, Joe R. 2006. *Systemic Racism: A Theory of Oppression*. New York: Routledge; Walker, David. 2000. *David Walker's Appeal to the Coloured Citizens of the World*, Peter P. Hinks, ed. University Park: Pennsylvania State University.

7. Tyler, Tom, and Cheryl J. Wakslak. 2004. "Profiling and Police Legitimacy: Procedural Justice, Attributions of Motive, and Acceptance of Police Authority." *Criminology* 42: 253–82, p. 253.

8. Brunson, Rod K. 2007. "'Police Don't Like Black People': African-American Young Men's Accumulated Police Experiences." *Criminology & Public Policy* 6: 71–101.

9. Russell, Katheryn K. 1998. *The Color of Crime: Racial Hoaxes, White Fear, Black Protectionism, Police Harassment, and Other Macroaggressions*. New York: New York University Press.

10. The *criminalblackman* is Russell's literary visual representing the amalgamation of the individual statuses of criminal, black, and man into one intersected identity. Russell, Katheryn K. 1998. *The Color of Crime*.

11. Buerger, Michael E., and Amy Farrell. 2002. "The Evidence of Racial Profiling: Interpreting Documented and Unofficial Sources." *Police Quarterly* 5: 272–305; Harris, David A. 2002. *Profiles in Injustice: Why Racial Profiling Cannot Work*. New York: New Press; Lamberth, John. 1998. *Driving While Black: A Statistician Proves That Prejudice Still Rules the Road*. Retrieved September 3, 2002. www.hartford-hwp.com/archives/45a/192.html; Ramirez, Deborah, Jack McDevitt, and Amy Farrell. 2000. "A Resource Guide on Racial Profiling Data Collection Systems: Promising Practices and Lessons Learned." Monograph. Washington, DC: U.S. Department of Justice; Russell, Katheryn K. 2001a. "Racial Profiling: A Status Report of the Legal, Legislative, and Empirical Literature." *Rutgers Race & The Law Review* 3: 61; Weitzer, Ronald, and Steven A. Tuch. 2004. "Race and Perceptions of Police Misconduct." *Social Problems* 51: 305–25; Withrow, Brian L. 2006. *Racial Profiling: From Rhetoric to Reason*. Upper Saddle River, NJ: Pearson-Prentice Hall.

12. Dunham, Roger G., Geoffrey P. Alpert, Meghan S. Stroshine, and Katherine Bennett. 2005. "Transforming Citizens into Suspects: Factors that Influence the Formation of Police Suspicion." *Police Quarterly* 8: 366–93; Parker, Karen F., John M. MacDonald, Geoffrey P. Alpert, Michael R. Smith, and Alex R. Piquero. 2004. "A Contextual Study of Racial Profiling: Assessing the Theoretical Rationale for the Study of Racial Profiling at the Local Level." *American Behavioral Scientist* 47: 943–62; Sampson, Robert J., and Dawn Jeglum Bartusch. 1998. "Legal Cynicism

and (Subcultural) Tolerance of Deviance: The Neighborhood Context of Racial Differences." *Law & Society Review* 32: 777–804; Tomaskovic-Devey, Donald, Marcinda Mason, and Matthew Zingraff. 2004. "Looking for the Driving While Black Phenomenon: Conceptualizing Racial Bias Processes and Their Associated Distributions." *Police Quarterly* 7: 3–29; Wilson, George, Roger Dunham, and Geoffrey Alpert. 2004. "Prejudice in Police Profiling: Assessing an Overlooked Aspect in Prior Research." *American Behavioral Scientist* 47: 896–909.

13. Weitzer and Tuch, *Race and Policing in America*.

14. Petrocelli, Matthew, Alex R. Piquero, and Michael R. Smith. 2003. "Conflict Theory and Racial Profiling: An Empirical Analysis of Police Traffic Stop Data." *Journal of Criminal Justice* 31: 1–11.

15. Weitzer, Ronald, and Steven A. Tuch. 2005. "Racially Biased Policing: Determinants of Citizen Perceptions." *Social Forces* 83: 1009–30.

16. Tomaskovic-Devey, Mason, and Zingraff, "Looking for the Driving While Black Phenomenon.

17. Wilson, Dunham, and Alpert, "Prejudice in Police Profiling."

18. Bonilla-Silva, *Racism without Racists*.

19. Parker, MacDonald, Alpert, Smith, and Piquero, "A Contextual Study of Racial Profiling"; Sampson and Bartusch, "Legal Cynicism and (Subcultural) Tolerance of Deviance."

20. Becker, Gary S. 1993. "Nobel Lecture: The Economic Way of Looking at Behavior." *Journal of Political Economy* 101: 385–409; Armour, Jody David. 1997. *Negrophobia and Reasonable Racism: The Hidden Costs of Being Black in America*. New York: New York University Press; Kennelly, Ivy. 1999. "'That Single-Mother Element': How White Employers Typify Black Women." *Gender and Society* 13: 168–92.

21. Engel, Robin Shepard, Jennifer M. Calnon, and Thomas J. Bernard. 2002. "Theory and Racial Profiling: Shortcomings and Future Directions in Research." *Justice Quarterly* 19: 249–73; Harris, *Profiles in Injustice*; MacDonald, Heather. 2003. *Are Cops Racist?* Chicago: Ivan R. Dee.

22. Russell, *The Color of Crime*, p. 39.

23. Lynch, Michael J., Danielle McGurrin, and Melissa Fenwick. 2004. "Disappearing Act: The Representation of Corporate Crime Research in Criminological Literature." *Journal of Criminal Justice* 32: 389–98.

24. Withrow, *Racial Profiling*.

25. Harcourt, Bernard E. 2007. *Against Prediction: Profiling, Policing, and Punishing in an Actuarial Age*. Chicago: University of Chicago Press. However, Harcourt's provocative analysis of racial profiling has been critiqued by Ariela Gross for his claim that "the problem with racial profiling is about the profiling, not about race." (p. 215) In the Winter 2008 issue (33/235) of *Law and Social Inquiry* dedicated to Harcourt's work, Gross comments: "I came away from his book convinced that we should tell this as a racial history as well. The history of actuarialism, I suspect, is also a history of racial thinking—that is, the same social scientists who focused on delinquency, parole, and criminology in this era were also developing new theories of race—environmentalist, to be sure, but heavily influenced by the racial science of the day." (p. 241)

26. Bennett, Gary G., Marcellus M. Merritt, Christopher L. Edwards and John J. Sollers III. 2004. "Perceived Racism and Affective Responses to Ambiguous

Interpersonal Interactions among African American Men." *American Behavioral Scientist* 47: 963–76; Tyler and Wakslak, "Profiling and Police Legitimacy; Weitzer, Ronald, and Steven A. Tuch. 1999. "Race, Class, and Perceptions of Discrimination by the Police." *Crime & Delinquency* 45: 494–507; Weitzer and Tuch, "Race and Perceptions of Police Misconduct."

27. Omi and Winant, *Racial Formation in the United States from the 1960s to the 1990s.*

28. Omi and Winant, *Racial Formation in the United States from the 1960s to the 1990s*, p. 56.

29. Weitzer, Ronald, and Steven A. Tuch. 2002. "Perceptions of Racial Profiling: Race, Class, and Personal Experience." *Criminology* 40: 435–56, p. 453.

30. Weitzer and Tuch, "Racially Biased Policing," p. 1011.

31. Weitzer and Tuch, "Racially Biased Policing," p. 1026 [italics mine].

32. Engel, Robin Shepard. 2005. "Citizens' Perceptions of Distributive and Procedural Injustice during Traffic Stops with Police." *Journal of Research in Crime and Delinquency* 42: 445–81.

33. Weitzer and Tuch, "Racially Biased Policing," pp. 1017 and 1025.

34. Tyler and Wakslak, "Profiling and Police Legitimacy," p. 253 [italics mine].

35. Zuberi, Tukufu, and Eduardo Bonilla-Silva. 2008. *White Logic, White Methods: Racism and Methodology*. Lanham, MD: Rowman & Littlefield.

36. Feagin, Joe R. 2006. *Systemic Racism: A Theory of Oppression*. New York: Routledge, p. 25.

37. Brown, Ben, and William Reed Benedict. 2002. "Perceptions of the Police: Past Findings, Methodological Issues, Conceptual Issues, and Policy Implications." *Policing: An International Journal of Police Strategies & Management* 25: 543–80; Weitzer and Tuch, "Racially Biased Policing."

38. Bonilla-Silva, Eduardo, and Gianpaolo Baiocchi. 2001. "Anything but Racism: How Sociologists Limit the Significance of Racism." *Race & Society* 4: 117–31; Feagin, Joe R. 2001. *Racist America: Roots, Current Realities, & Future Reparations*. New York: Routledge.

39. Weitzer and Tuch, *Race and Policing in America.*

40. Weitzer and Tuch, *Race and Policing in America*, p. 180.

41. Weitzer and Tuch, *Race and Policing in America*, p. 204. For rare qualitative work, see also Weitzer, Ronald. 2000. "Racialized Policing: Residents' Perceptions in Three Neighborhoods." *Law & Society Review* 34: 129–55.

42. A combination some consider antithetical to Blumer's theoretical spirit, see Esposito, Luigi, and John W. Murphy. 1999. "Desensitizing Herbert Blumer's Work on Race Relations: Recent Applications of His Group Position Theory to the Study of Contemporary Racial Prejudice." *Sociological Quarterly* 40: 397–410.

43. Bonilla-Silva, *Racism without Racists.*

44. Wilson, Dunham, and Alpert, "Prejudice in Police Profiling."

45. Feagin, *Racist America.*

46. Bonilla-Silva, "Rethinking Racism," p. 467.

47. Bonilla-Silva, "Rethinking Racism"; Feagin, *Systemic Racism.*

48. Zuberi, Tukufu. 2001. *Thicker Than Blood: How Racial Statistics Lie*. Minneapolis: University of Minnesota Press.

49. Bonilla-Silva, "Rethinking Racism."
50. Weitzer and Tuch, "Racially Biased Policing"; Bennett, Merritt, Edwards, and Sollers, "Perceived Racism and Affective Responses to Ambiguous Interpersonal Interactions among African American Men."
51. Weitzer and Tuch, "Race, Class, and Perceptions of Discrimination by the Police."
52. Wilson, William Julius. 1978. *The Declining Significance of Race: Blacks and Changing American Institutions*. Chicago: University of Chicago Press.
53. Feagin, Joe R., and Melvin P. Sikes. 1994. *Living with Racism: The Black Middle-Class Experience*. Boston: Beacon Press; Hagan and Albonetti, "Race, Class, and the Perception of Criminal Injustice in America."
54. Cited in Bonilla-Silva, *Racism without Racist*, p. 98.
55. Tyler and Wakslak, "Profiling and Police Legitimacy. " p. 252.
56. Engel, "Citizens' Perceptions of Distributive and Procedural Injustice during Traffic Stops with Police."
57. Engel, "Citizens' Perceptions of Distributive and Procedural Injustice during Traffic Stops with Police," p. 464.
58. Piquero, Alex R., Zenta Gomez-Smith, and Lynn Langton. 2004. "Discerning Unfairness Where Others May Not: Low Self-Control and Unfair Sanction Perceptions." *Criminology* 42: 699–733.
59. Bonilla-Silva, "Rethinking Racism," p. 467.
60. Bell, Derrick. 1992. *Faces at the Bottom of the Well: The Permanence of Racism*. New York: Basic Books, p. 198.
61. Reitzel, John D., Stephen K. Rice, and Alex R. Piquero. 2004. "Lines and Shadows: Perceptions of Racial Profiling and the Hispanic Experience." *Journal of Criminal Justice* 32: 607–16.
62. Weitzer and Tuch, "Perceptions of Racial Profiling," p. 437.
63. Reitzel, John D., and Alex R. Piquero. 2006. "Does It Exist? Studying Citizens' Attitudes of Racial Profiling." *Police Quarterly* 9: 161–83.
64. Bonilla-Silva, *Racism without Racists*, p. 11.
65. Weitzer and Tuch, "Racially Biased Policing," p. 1014.
66. Bonilla-Silva, *Racism without Racists*.
67. Bonilla-Silva, *Racism without Racists*.
68. Bonilla-Silva, *Racism without Racists*, p. 61.

4

Critical Race Methodology and Race Theory

> The goal of critical race theory is . . . to identify race as a central rather than marginal factor in defining and explaining individual experiences of the law. By acknowledging racism as the overarching affliction of the American legal system, we may begin to explore the more complex dynamics embodied in facially neutral rules, institutions, and attitudes. Toward that end, attention to differences of racial perspective is not just helpful, but necessary.
>
> Katheryn Russell-Brown[1]

In this chapter I have two primary goals. First is to demonstrate the need for qualitative examinations in racial profiling research as a contrast to the quantitative, heavy state of affairs in mainstream criminology. Specifically, a critical race methodology[2] is inherently about the importance of the narrative in illuminating raced social phenomenon as it allows social actors to reflect and represent social experiences on their own terms. The counter narrative, a staple of critical theory, is used to contest dominant representations of social phenomenon. While my work focuses on the relationship of the narrative to a critical *race* framework, the importance of the narrative transcends concerns with race alone, as the narrative has long been a method of illumination in feminist, postmodern, critical gender, and critical class theory, as well as the intersectionality of these constructs.[3] My second goal is to contextualize racial profiling within race theory and within Foucault's important conceptualization of panopticonism[4] for additional framing of social control and domination in the racial realm.

Criminology has long engaged the race–crime nexus, sometimes forwarding the construct of race-as-biology as in Lombroso's criminal man theorization, while at other times the criminological realm has served as a "site for resistance to the conscious or unconscious reproduction of racism in both society and scholarship."[5] For an example of the latter, DuBois was a pioneer in contextualizing (street) crime rates as a function of sociospatial concerns, resource allocation, and society's emphasis on particular *forms* of crime over others.[6] In a recent review of critical criminological insights on race, class, and gender, Gregg Barak et al. offer a number of examples of how mainstream criminology, even in some classic theoretical studies, did indeed complicate the racial minority and crime connection in the face of dominant discourses and social practices that positioned racial minority status as an inferior status.[7] Complicating dominant representations is a defining characteristic of *critical* criminology even if it is not labeled as such.[8]

A CRITICAL RACE METHODOLOGY

One major component of critical analysis is to challenge traditional ways of examining oppression while engaging in work that is liberative and transformative.[9] As described by Kimberlé Crenshaw, one of the founders of the critical race theory movement:

> Critical race theory . . . is unified by two common interests. The first is to understand how a regime of white supremacy and its subordination of people of color have been created and maintained in America, and, in particular, to examine the relationship between that social structure and professed ideals such as "the rule of law" and "equal protection." The second is a desire not merely to understand the vexed bond between law and racial power but to *change* it.[10]

Because qualitative methodology is a vastly underutilized methodology in mainstream criminology, the use of it in this book serves the purpose of critical analysis to challenge the approaches—guided by white logic—that establish the knowledge academia and the public have about this important social phenomenon. The *nature* of people's experiences is best captured in qualitative research.[11] As discussed by Anselm Strauss and Juliet Corbin,[12] qualitative research is:

> any type of research that produces findings not arrived at by statistical procedures or other means of quantification. It can refer to research about persons' lives, lived experiences, behaviors, emotions, and feelings. . . . In speaking about qualitative analysis, we are referring not to the quantifying

> of qualitative data but rather to a nonmathematical process of interpretation, carried out for the purpose of discovering concepts and relationships in raw data and then organizing these into a theoretical explanatory scheme.

I specifically engage a critical race methodology—a form of scholarship emerging from critical race theory—as conceptualized by Daniel Solorzano and Tara Yosso.[13] These education scholars offer several propositions for a critical race methodology approach. First, a race lens is critical to every aspect of the research process. Second, traditional ways of viewing the issue at hand—here, racial profiling—are challenged. Third, the research process is driven by efforts at liberation and transformation. Fourth, the *experiences* of communities of color are central to the process and viewed as bases of power. Last, sources of knowledge used to inform the research process are varied and critically oriented. In sum, critical race methodology is directed research "grounded in the experiences and knowledge of people of color."[14]

A central tenet of any critical theory is the naming of one's own reality by use of narratives to counter suppositions about social matters forwarded through hegemonic discourses. Storytelling and counter stories (those narratives directly contradicting dominant assumptions) have long been a practice in African American and Latino communities.[15] Critical race theory is intended to present storytelling and narratives as "valid approaches through which to examine race and racism in the law and society."[16] This is methodological contestation to the white logic orientation that has traditionally discounted qualitative work, frequently in the discursive form that typifies it as anecdotal. Qualitative research is also frequently critiqued for the relatively small number (a reference to quantitative work and a reflection of white logic in itself) of respondents that a typical analysis engages—perhaps only ten to fifteen respondents.[17] Yet the beauty of a qualitative project is that even within a relatively short segment of data, there are a number of "data points."[18]

A 2004 study by leading police studies researchers on perceptions of police misconduct offers insight on the quantitative and qualitative divide.[19] The survey-based study included over 1,700 respondents. Respondents were asked, for example, "how often do you think police officers stop people in your neighborhood/city without good reason—never, on occasion, fairly often, or very often," and "have you ever been stopped on the street by the police for no reason?" The authors conclude that communities of color were more likely to respond in the "often" range and with a positive answer, respectively. This survey analysis shows a link between racial status and views of policing practices, and thus is important knowledge in our efforts to understand how racial status operates in the criminal justice realm. However, it does not engage what it is about the nature of the policing practices and why the experience is meaningful. Qualitative work is able to get at the context, meaning, and experiential quality of these relations.

Criminology and racial/ethnic studies have their share of important research studies that relied upon one or a small number of respondents for illumination of a particular subject. For example, Clifford Shaw's 1930 book *The Jack-Roller* chronicled the experiences of one juvenile delinquent and is viewed as an informative work in social science research.[20] Shaw, from the iconic Chicago School, was later recognized for his development of the now-classic social disorganization theory in partnership with Henry McKay (a theory that to a degree countered dominant perspectives about crime and race because of its sociospatial orientation contextualizing criminal offending).[21] William Chambliss's 1973 *The Saints and the Roughnecks* was an ethnography based on fourteen youths and is considered an essential work in introductory courses in criminology today. This work in particular helped usher in a growing critical orientation to the discipline of criminology.[22] Carl Klockar's 1974 book *The Professional Fence* is another now-classic study in criminology whose focus was one individual who offered insight on the broker component of stolen goods trafficking.[23] Klockars is now recognized as one of the early scholars in police studies. In racial/ethnic studies, the ground-breaking work of Ruth Frankenberg in her 1993 *White Women, Race Matters: The Social Construction of Whiteness* was based, for example, on only thirty respondents.[24] This book ushered in what is now a developed area of race studies on whiteness. I suggest that one of the reasons why these works were successful and viewed as quality scholarship is because the experiential quality of each, when contextualized within existing knowledge, are indeed authentic in their representations—however limited the sample.

Both sides of the quantitative–qualitative "divide" help explain racial dynamics. Qualitative work is valid not because it can be quantified; it is valid because it engages the voices of those social actors involved in social processes and allows them to "evaluate, interpret, and respond" to issues via their own assessments.[25] These responses provide meaning and depth to our understandings of social processes.

One informative distinction between qualitative and quantitative work is that of similarity or transferability versus representativeness. In his review of Herbert Blumer's work on the "sensitizing concept," Will van den Hoonaard suggests that qualitative researchers are most interested in "establishing an empirical *similarity* of their cases," while quantitative researchers are concerned that their findings are representative of the population as a whole and thus are "striving for generalizations" beyond their sample.[26] My methodological orientation is also guided in part by Michael Burawoy's notion of the extended case method as it is concerned with the context of meaning and the macro determinants of everyday life. Specifically, Burawoy views the extended case method as an effort to take "the social situation as the point of empirical examination and works with given general concepts and laws about states, economies, legal orders, and the like to understand how those micro situations are shaped by wider structures."[27] This orientation is appropriate in my analysis as narratives are accounts of the everyday that reflect larger forces in society.

Narrative analysis, even of relatively limited data, is key to critical theory as it is "a method for eliciting and empowering rarely heard perspectives from subordinated communities."[28] Critical-oriented work that seeks to generate insight and explain circumstances is also concerned with "unmasking dominant, social structures and the vested interests they represent, with a goal of transforming society and freeing individuals from the sources of domination and repression."[29] Critical race methodology concerns a rearticulation of the social science paradigm that posits the researcher as "objective cartographer of knowledge" personified in the positivist tradition of quantification and instead affords "minoritized bodies possibilities for narrating [and] naming our oppressions and strategies for resistance/survival."[30] Traditional examinations of race and crime come from the dominant group perspective and "reproduces dominant ideology by studying subordinate groups as a 'problem' rather than as people with agency. . . ."[31]

POLITICS OF RESEARCH

Social science research is a political enterprise."[32] Noted qualitative authority Yvonna Lincoln[33] explains how this political orientation in the research process is now negotiated, yet still positions research that is not openly articulated as political (note the reference to "disengaged academic") as relatively neutral (an example of a white logic orientation, even by a researcher who has done a great deal to validate qualitative research in the social sciences):

> The desire to create change, to lessen oppression, or to assist in the development of a more equitable world sets up a different research dynamic from that of the disengaged academic whose main purpose is to add to the stock of theoretical knowledge. And if we are to raise such issues about the research process, then the manner in which we present data, and to whom, also comes under renewed scrutiny.

Critical race theory is bound to the idea that the experiential understanding of communities of color about how race operates is valid and legitimate, with the process of interpreting data being described as "the interplay between researchers and data."[34] This premise acknowledges the influence of the researcher on the research project, specifically the politics and interpretation that the researcher brings to the work and openly addresses. Further, in acknowledging the inherent subjectivity and political nature of social science, I agree with Bonilla-Silva's assessment that "pure objectivity, the problems we pose, the theories we use, the methods we employ, and the analyses we perform are social products themselves and to an extent reflect societal contractions and power dynamics."[35]

CONTEXTUALIZING RACIAL PROFILING IN RACE THEORY AND SOCIAL CONTROL THEORY

I argue that the neglect of mainstream criminologists to adequately contextualize racial profiling processes in *theory* has allowed public understanding (especially for whites) of the phenomenon to remain one primarily of crime control rather than, as I argue, one of racial oppression. Racial profiling studies are recognized, even by those in the field, as lacking a theoretical foundation. In the rare instances that *race* theory is engaged, that theory is inadequate for understanding the operation of race in contemporary times because of its individual, micro-level orientation. Traditional race theory perspectives often focus on assimilation and contact phenomenon.[36] These perspectives focused on individual-level concerns and on an adoption of dominant group values for the racial order to change to any significant degree. Thus the elimination of racial oppression depended on the elimination of racially oppressing actors, with social institutions and embedded racist practices inherent to those institutions in society getting a relative pass on their ability to influence society's racial order. As argued by Omi and Winant,[37] traditional race theories:

> neglect both the institutional and ideological nature of race in America, and the systemic presence of racial dynamics in such social spheres as education, art, social policy, law, religion, and science. Instead, they focus attention on racial dynamics as the irrational products of individual pathologies. Such assumptions make it impossible to grasp the specificity of racism and racial conflict in the U.S.

Similarly, as discussed by Bonilla-Silva:[38]

> from a structural point of view, race relations are not rooted in the balance between "good" (nonracist) and "bad" (racist) whites or even in the struggle between "racist" actors (conscious of their racial interest) and "race militants" (conscious of the need to oppose the racial status quo). The reproduction of racial inequality transpires every day through the normal operation

> of society. Like capitalists and men, whites have been able to crystallize their victories in institutions and practices. This implies that they do not need to be *individually* active in the maintenance of racial domination.

The importance of examining racial processes within a theoretical framework specifically addressing race seems commonsensical. Yet, very little attention is paid to race in and of itself in current studies addressing racial profiling (which may be explained in part by the demographic make-up of those scholars). Race scholars Omi and Winant[39] argue that without a firm grounding of the concept and operation of race, analysis of the social world is difficult:

> Until we understand the concept of race, it is impossible effectively to analyze the familiar issues which involve race. It is hard to grasp the way racial identity is assigned and assumed, or to perceive the tacit racial dimensions of everyday experience, for example, without a clear sense of the socially constructed meaning of race. Similarly, without an awareness that the concept of race is subject to permanent political contestation, it is difficult to recognize the enduring role race plays in the social structure—in organizing social inequalities of various sorts, in shaping the very geography of American life, in framing political initiatives and state action.

In this chapter, I lay out several theoretical frameworks that allow for a more comprehensive understanding of racialized law enforcement and related practices of the *racial state*. Racial profiling is a complex issue. It involves the intersection of racial and ethnic status, social control, and the state. Because I argue that racial profiling is an issue of racial oppression from the state, critical race theory constructs from Bonilla-Silva, Collins, DuBois, Feagin, Omi and Winant, and Russell dominate my race theory analysis and/or operate as guiding constructs throughout the book. In my qualitative analysis, I engage theory about social control from Foucault and his conception of panopticonism as well.

The canvas of criminology is white. Borrowing from Alford Young[40] and France Winddance Twine and Jonathan Warren,[41] I attempt to provide an alternative portrait of the racial profiling landscape in criminology by "racing" the racial profiling research via a centering of the phenomenon within a racial oppression context. This follows a tradition in criminology, particularly over the past two decades, to engage "a variety of race, gender, and hybrid analyses of crime and justice, such as those involving feminist perspectives" to provoke scholarship within the discipline into marginalized social realms.[42] The one I forward here specifically in regards to the racial profiling literature in mainstream criminology is inspired by Russell's "ethical imperative"[43] and Zuberi and Bonilla-Silva's call for serious activist-oriented assessment of processes in the production and dissemination of knowledge that reproduce racial inequality:

> Critical social scientists on race matters can provide data, arguments, counternarratives, and all sorts of intellectual ammunition against dominant representations about racial groups and racial inequality. And to provide better ammunition for the movements against White supremacy, the sociological and social scientific efforts in this field must be race conscious and engage in a systematic analysis of racial stratification and its effects.[44]

Theoretical frameworks from Bonilla-Silva and Omi and Winant discussed thus far have underscored the importance of viewing race as part of the normal operation and arrangement of the racial state. Feagin also forces examination of race as structural and systemic to American society. At the beginning of his book, *Systemic Racism: A Theory of Oppression*, Feagin asks "What are the distinctive social worlds that have been created by racial oppression over several centuries?"[45] He argues that because racism is more than "racial prejudice and individual bigotry. . . [but] material, social, and ideological reality that is well-embedded in major U.S. institutions," it is *systemic* in United States society. Feagin asserts that all racial–ethnic relationships and events need be contextualized within this systemic understanding of racial oppression. The *everydayness* of racial profiling is critical to understanding the cumulative racial processes and effects that manifest in social institutions such as the criminal justice system.

Situating racial profiling processes within the systemic racism realm works because this theory suggests that a "recurring exercise of coercive power" is necessary for the operation of racial oppression.[46] The regularity of racial profiling as a social phenomenon—in the form of racial minority overrepresentation in traffic stops and associated processes—is now well documented. Systemic racism is also appropriate as a theoretical guide because of its emphasis on the separating, distancing, and alienating relations that emerge under racial systems—what I refer to as a break from citizenship in my analysis of the dominant narrative of citizenship. As well, Feagin uses a *white racial frame* metaphor as a theoretical tool for explicating systemic racism. He defines this concept as "an organized set of racialized ideas, stereotypes, emotions, and inclinations to discriminate . . . [that] generates . . . recurring and habitual discriminatory actions" manifesting in the routine activities of social institutions.[47] Clearly, racial profiling processes emerge from these racialized ideas, stereotypes, and inclinations at social control via the legal realm.

Readers familiar with Feagin's works know his orientation that any discussion of racial oppression is not complete until there is an accompanying discussion of resistance to oppression. Thus, systemic racism theory incorporates a component of resistance to further understand the experiences of those oppressed. His initial discussion of resistance as a countering force to racial oppression underscores the adaptive nature of resistance as the formation of oppression has changed over the centuries. In chapter 6 of my analysis, resistance is a central topic of examination. In conjunction with Collins's work in *Black Feminist Thought*[48] in which she examines various formations of resistance (discussed below), my examination of the experiences of people of color with racial profiling follows these theoretical frameworks that oppressive practices are met with resistance. This is in line with Feagin's assertion that "the very people whose racially oppressed condition had been guaranteed by white leaders in several provisions of the founding Constitution were those who most forthrightly asserted the high ideals of equality, liberty, and justice. . . ."[49]

COLLECTIVE MEMORY, "THE LESSON" AND LIVED EXPERIENCE

Another theoretical alignment with systemic racism theory in the current study is a variation of what Feagin and others refer to as *collective memory*. As discussed in the preceding chapter, my intent is to critically explore one of the main areas of examination in the current racial profiling literature—that is, the influence of vicarious experience in shaping perceptions of racial profiling. As discussed more thoroughly in chapter 6, I use the conception of *the lesson* to explain the informational exchange process where generally elderly people of color pass on critical insight to younger generations about how to negotiate in a racial state.[50] Collective memory is a more expansive phenomenon than the lesson, as it encompasses a greater myriad of historical contexts for understanding experiences of communities of color. The lesson, as engaged here, is targeted more toward specific coercive encounters with the state. I argue that from a critical race perspective, there is a subtext in the current literature's focus on *vicarious experience*. For example, vicarious experience includes what leading racial profiling scholars have described as an "amplified" affect—read *exaggerated* affect—on personal experience.[51] This characterization differs from more critical formulations where they view the passing on of information as crucial to community negotiation of the color line. As stated by Feagin:[52]

> One of the mechanisms important to the social reproduction of systemic racism, as well as for the reproduction of resistance, is collective memory . . . [when people of color] discuss or allude to the importance of young people being taught about white-on-black oppression. Older black Americans recount or imply the importance of collective memories indicating lessons, for young and old, on what past oppression was like and on how to respond when it crashes into an individual's or a family's life in the present.

I make a theoretical distinction between the current literature's vicarious experience and what more critical insight offers and conceptualizes as collective memory or the lesson. The latter views these processes as social incorporation of a "fundamental stock of knowledge needed to cope in everyday situations: the ways to move about and survive in hostile social worlds."[53] Again, the lesson, as it is used in the current work, refers to advice and admonition about encounters with law enforcement and reflects a more complex understanding of the informational exchange about law enforcement in communities of color than is portrayed in the body of work on racial profiling now available. This framework is in line with my respondents' contexualization of racial profiling within larger social realms. It is not simply the act of the traffic stop but what the act represents in these larger experiential realms. The experience is "interpreted on the basis of knowledge gained from previous events as well as from the collective knowledge. . . ."[54]

In sum, Feagin's work is useful for a theoretical guide because it addresses the fundamental nature of racial oppression as it occurs in the everyday, thus making the experiential quality of narrative examinations like the current study crucial to understanding racial oppression. Furthermore, Feagin's concentration on resistance to racial oppression helps frame, along with Collins's work, modes of opposition that emerge in the face of racial oppression.

DUBOIS AND FOUCAULT: CULTIVATING AWARENESS OF SOCIAL CONTROL

To get at the fundamental nature of racism in the normal and everyday operations of America, I engage the work of DuBois[55] and Foucault[56] to get insight into the effects of everyday racial oppressions on people of color who have been racially profiled. Specifically, I engage the work of these two distinct social theorists to frame racial profiling as an issue of power, hypersurveillance, and marginalization. I also contextualize DuBois's work as resistance to racial oppression following Collins's argument that *critical awareness* of racial oppression is in itself resistance to it.

Racial profiling processes, I argue, offer an example of how informal historical and contemporary racial paradigms and practices of society and the state affect citizenship. Surveillance is about identity. Notions of *who belongs where* have long organized policies in racialized states such as the United States, through institutionalized slavery and Native American dissemination experiences to historical and contemporary immigration debates.[57] Identity imposed by the state during racial profiling processes involve the criminalization of citizens. While DuBois was at the fore of contextualizing issues of crime and social control within the bounds of a racial state, with notable exceptions largely from African American scholars, his work has not been engaged to explain these matters.[58] DuBois's concept of *double consciousness* refers to an awareness one has and cultivates that recognizes the magnitude of status and identity concerns in a racially ordered society. Fundamentally, it is a concept to understand how racialization processes influence those who are subjected to racial and other oppressions. What are the mechanisms that emerge to deal with, contextualize, and resist racial oppression?

As described by DuBois: "One ever feels his two-ness,—an American, a Negro; two souls, two thoughts, two unreconciled strivings; two warring ideals in one dark body, whose dogged strength alone keeps it from being torn asunder."[59] The sense of "two-ness" described by DuBois is a direct reference to the limits of citizenship in practice for people of color when they confront, with varying modes of resistance, the social fact of racialized citizenship emergent through surveillance processes of the state. Racial minority identity, often hypervisible through racialization and criminalization processes like racial profiling, is not reconciled with citizenship identity in the eyes of many whites. This contradiction between identifying as a person of color yet having full citizenship denied—in the wake of public discourse proclaiming equal treatment under the law—creates awareness of racial power dynamics. In chapter 6, I expand on DuBois's work as it specifically applies to the qualitative analysis of in-depth interviews with people of color who have been racially profiled.

In addition to DuBois's work, I extend Foucault's concept of the panopticon to contextualize racial profiling processes and effects as surveillance-based social control systems. The panopticon is a social control mechanism introduced by social theorist Jeremy Bentham in the 1800s as part of his prison reform efforts. The basic design is a circular prison complex with a tower in the center of the structure. The inmates reside in the cells that face outward to the central tower and, because of architectural/interior design that includes backlighting of each cell, monitoring of inmates is facilitated. A key aspect of the panopticon experience, however, is that the inmates need not *always* be under surveillance in order for social control to occur once they have been exposed experientially to the surveillance. Consequently, according to Foucault, a self-monitoring and self-consciousness occurs with the inmates. In essence, these individuals experience being under suspicion by authorities at all times. Foucault explains:[60]

> the major effect of the panopticon: to induce in the inmate a sense of conscious and permanent visibility that assures the automatic functioning of power . . . the surveillance is permanent in its effects, even if it is discontinuous

> in its action; that the perfection of power should tend to render its actual exercise unnecessary.

The "permanent visibility" of race as a functioning marker of criminality and the permanent visibility induced by the panopticon—always being under suspicion—are similar. An *automatic functioning of power* develops as the individual—here, the citizen of color—is reminded of the power relationship they are in with the state.

Foucault saw the move to what he termed discipline power of the state as a shift away from overt and more conventional forms of social control. He suggests mental coercion may be more socially harmful than traditional social control efforts:[61]

> there is a shift in the point of application of this power: it is no longer the body, with the ritual play of excessive pains, spectacular brandings in the ritual of the public execution; it is the mind or rather a play of representations and signs circulating discreetly but necessarily and evidently in the minds of all. It is no longer the body, but the soul.

Surveillance processes by the state such as racial profiling provide a contemporary example. No longer are most race-based restrictions about *who belongs where* promulgated through official state-sanctioned policies. Racial profiling, with its somewhat elusive character, emerges in the contemporary era as a way to govern racially without reliance on more overt forms of racial governance. The move from the body to the mind/soul is representative of a move from more overt forms of racial oppression to more covert formations in the contemporary era, which is in line with other examinations of racialization processes in the post-Civil Rights era.[62]

It is useful to engage the works of DuBois and Foucault on the issue of racial profiling because each expresses a concern with the effects of constant surveillance and evaluation on the individual, in addition to acknowledging how these surveillance and criminalization processes are tools of the (racial) state.

For DuBois, this concern manifests in the double-consciousness concept where individuals of color recognize the ramifications of racial/ethnic status in determining how far citizenship rights and protections are extended, both for themselves and for whites. The recognition that full citizenship is generally excluded from their experience in a white-dominated social realm, particularly in the face of public discourse that may fervently suggest otherwise, offers people of color unique insight into the racial state that whites do not possess.[63] Experiential knowledge that the use of racial status is employed as a tool of the state when making assumptions of criminality provides an example of the limitations of equal protection under the law discourse that is fundamental to double-consciousness awareness.

At a basic level, Foucault's panopticonism concerns social control. The panopticon effect—where individuals have an awareness of constant monitoring, patrolling, and surveillance—induces an awareness of power relations with the state. Thus the panoptic effect also involves an awareness of oppression, similar in process to DuBois's double consciousness. For instance, when one of my respondents comments on the regularity of racialization and criminalization processes evident in the racial profiling phenomenon, I consider this as part of the panopticon effect and a reflection of double consciousness. I offer more discussion of Foucault in chapter 7 on vicarious experience.

RESISTANCE TO RACIAL OPPRESSION

As described by Feagin, investigation of racial oppression, of which the current work accepts as a premise of racial profiling processes, must include examination of the constant resistance when communities of color "counter, restructure, and overturn" societal oppression.[64]

To examine resistance, I engage Collins's monumental work *Black Feminist Thought* and extend her ideas on black women's resistance to racism and sexism into the citizen–state realm that encompasses racial profiling processes. Collins's work is appropriate because she frames oppression as an issue of surveillance with a focus on the rejection of what she calls "controlling identities."[65] Surveillance and the rejection of *criminalizing* identities is fundamentally a part of the racial profiling realm when examined through the lens of resistance. The intersectionality that Collins's work is concerned with—that is, the interlapping identities of race, gender, and sexuality, among others—points to this broader concern of critical studies and more holistic approaches to understanding the structural forms of oppression.[66] The integrated approach forwarded by Barak et al. looks to the varied manifestations in which class, race, and gender collectively structure people's actions and others' reactions to them and how "these hierarchies are used to either sustain or resist the prevailing systems of inequality and privilege."[67]

Collins describes how acts of resistance manifest in both direct and indirect confrontations with power. Her work is also important because she not only examines resistance as direct confrontations with "institutional power," but also examines less obvious forms of resistance in what she calls "struggles for group survival" as equally meaningful strategies of resistance to oppression.[68] Among these, in the analysis to follow, concerns DuBois's idea that the awareness of racial oppression in and of itself indicates a critical consciousness—a privileged critical consciousness that reflects resistance.

A guiding research inquiry in my analysis is what are the forms of resistance that emerge during or following a racialized traffic stop? The most obvious form of resistance is described by Collins as a direct confrontation with institutional power.[69] She argues that this mode of resistance has been historically off-limits to black women because of their lack of access to institutions and traditional realms of activism like labor unions and the political arena. Similarly, I argue, communities of color have been historically denied access to the law enforcement realm and have suffered as a main target of law enforcement practices. Direct confrontations with the institution of the police force historically and even contemporarily could result in death. Collins argues that more covert forms of resistance emerge when conditions are too perilous to make direct confrontations with power, and that traditional examinations of political resistance do not always recognize such varied forms of resistance. Part of the struggle for group survival includes "crafting political strategies" that privilege critical consciousness in the face of racial oppression.[70] This theoretical perspective is highly useful in examining the interviews in later chapters and demonstrates the danger people of color—particularly young men of color—face in the post-Civil Rights era.

As noted, the most overt form of resistance in Collins's work is the direct confrontation with institutional power. I consider any discussion of going through "formal channels" as an example of a direct confrontation with institutional power. It includes, for example, asking for a supervisor during or following the traffic stop encounter and/or requesting written documentation of the stop. The latter issue, the demand for a citation when none might not otherwise be given, is an interesting dimension of resistance to racial profiling. By some accounts, when a person of color is detained but then ultimately let off without formal documentation of a violation, it may be supportive of initial indications the citizen had about racialization.[71] While whites may even boast about getting out of a ticket, the experience for many people of color is different.

The second strategy is a rejection of white supremacy ideology and the assumption that whiteness equals authority, knowledge, power, and truth. The strategy comes up in various forms from the respondents when they reject ruling ideologies and racial assumptions of power. I include in this category of resistance instances when the respondents themselves overtly call law enforcement on the racialized practice taking place. This incorporates a rejection of the criminal identity that is imposed on the person of color during a traffic stop. Not only is the criminal identity denied, thus indicating a rejection of the state's ability to ideologically shape one's self-concept, but many of the respondents engage in credentialing—an offering of self-assessments—to demonstrate their connection to the citizen ideal.

Respondents assess their experiences on their own terms, evaluate the circumstances, and contextualize how it connects to larger issues of dominance in their lives through self-defining and self-valuing strategies. Self-definition and self-valuation may include what has elsewhere been referred to as "role flexing."[72] These concepts include instances where people of color are aware of racial oppression but limit their outward rejection of the oppression in order to have control in the situation. Although role flexibility may be viewed as accommodation or capitulation to the racial oppression, Collins's argument is that *playing the game* is indeed a form of resistance when there is critical consciousness of the situation. In the racial profiling realm, as noted earlier, "doing what you have to do" to get yourself out of a given situation is in practical terms an issue of group survival for communities of color over the centuries.

Another dimension of resistance is producing "tangible, political changes" in others' lives, in addition to their own.[73] In the racial profiling resistance realm, this encompasses, among other things, efforts to become more informed about law enforcement, offering guidance ("the lesson") within their social networks about how to deal with law enforcement encounters, and making a call to others to resist forms of oppression in their own lives.

One of the most powerful tactics of resistance discussed by Collins has a long history in the literature on resistance: the idea that personal issues that "crash in on" the everyday are, for marginalized communities, political manifestations of oppression. Collins refers to this as "personal troubles" being "politically constituted."[74] Part of classic feminist theory, this component is clearly related to citizenship discourse. It concerns one's awareness of how the larger social context influences personal experiences. It points to a collective conscious that marks citizenship. Those instances where my respondents make reference to communities of color as a collective, and the collective impact that racialization and criminalization processes have on them as a whole are considered under this framework. Resistance to limited citizenship is part and parcel of the police–minority relationship.

Tara Yosso and David Garcia also offer an explication of varied modes of resistance, including their arrangement of *resistant capital* that was developed in response to Pierre Bourdieu's classic and they argue *flawed* conception of cultural capital.[75] Ross Haenfler, in his examination of subcultural resistance, suggests "at the individual level, resistance entails staking out an individual identity and asserting subjectivity in an adversarial context. In addition . . . individualized resistance is symbolic of a larger collective oppositional consciousness."[76] In practice, confrontations with institutional power—here the state—coalesce with more subtle forms of resistance. Paths to resistance are many: informal, formal, fluid, and intersectional. As put by Collins, if "power as domination is organized and operates via intersecting oppressions, then resistance must show comparable complexity."[77]

CONCLUSION

In this chapter, I stipulate that a critical theoretical and methodological approach to understanding racial profiling in the contemporary era is necessary to deepen our understanding of these racializing and criminalizing processes. In the two data chapters that comprise Part III of this book, I refer back to some of these theoretical constructs from race and social control scholarship to aid the reader in my assessments of the data. At times, I introduce new dimensions of the theoretical frameworks to show the complexities of racial profiling processes. One of my primary critiques of the current literature is that it concentrates on the bounded police–minority relationship, that is, it focuses on the individuals involved and neglects broader sociolegal realms. This critique is affirmed in the examinations to follow with the emergence of what I consider the dominant narrative of my analysis—that of the salience of citizenship rights and protections. Because of the salience of citizenship in the narratives examined in chapters 6 and 7, I offer the following brief chapter on citizenship constructs.

NOTES

1. Russell, Katheryn K. 2001b. "Development of a Black Criminology and the Role of the Black Criminologist." Pp. 279–92 in *African American Classics in Criminology & Criminal Justice*, Shaun L. Gabbidon, Helen Taylor Greene, and Vernetta D. Young, eds. Thousand Oaks, CA: Sage Publications.

2. Solorzano, Daniel G., and Tara J. Yosso. 2002. "Critical Race Methodology: Counter-storytelling as an Analytical Framework for Education Research." *Qualitative Inquiry* 8: 23–44.

3. Barak, Gregg, Jeanne Flavin, and Paul Leighton. 2007. *Class, Race, Gender, and Crime: The Social Realities of Justice in America*. Lanham, MD: Rowman & Littlefield; Davis, Angela Y. 1983. *Women, Race, and Class*. New York: Vintage Books; Marchetti, Elena. 2008. "Intersectional Race and Gender Analyses: Why Legal Processes Just Don't Get It." *Social Legal Studies* 1: 155–74; Lynch, Michael J. 1996. "Class, Race, Gender and Criminology: Structured Choices and the Life

Course." Pp. 3–28 in *Race, Gender, and Class in Criminology: The Intersection*. Martin D. Schwartz and Dragan Milovanovic, eds. New York: Garland.

4. Foucault, Michel. 1977. *Discipline & Punish: The Birth of the Prison*. (Translated by Alan Sheridan). New York: Random House.

5. Barak, Flavin, and Leighton, p. 105.

6. Katz, Michael B., and Thomas J. Sugrue, eds. 1998. *W.E.B. DuBois, Race, and the City: The Philadelphia Negro and Its Legacy*. Philadelphia: University of Pennsylvania Press.

7. Barak, Flavin, and Leighton, *Class, Race, Gender, and Crime*.

8. Lanier, Mark M., and Stuart Henry. 2004. *Essential Criminology*. Boulder, CO: Westview Press.

9. Solorzano and Yosso, "Critical Race Methodology."

10. Crenshaw, Kimberlé, Neil Gotanda, Gary Peller, and Kendall Thomas. 1995. *Critical Race Theory: The Key Writings that Informed the Movement*. New York: New Press, p. xiii.

11. Jamal, Samina. 2005. "Critical Ethnography." Pp. 225–40 in *Critical Issues in Anti-Racist Research Methodologies*, George J. Sefa Dei and Gurpreet Singh Johal, eds. New York: Peter Lang Publishing.

12. Strauss, Anselm, and Juliet Corbin. 1998. *Basics of Qualitative Research: Techniques and Procedures for Developing Grounded Theory*. Thousand Oaks, CA: Sage Publications, p. 10.

13. Solorzano and Yosso, "Critical Race Methodology."

14. Solorzano and Yosso, p. 23.

15. Bell, Derrick. 1992. *Faces at the Bottom of the Well: The Permanence of Racism*. New York: Basic Books; Delgado, Rodrigo and Jean Stefancic, eds. 2000. *Critical Race Theory: The Cutting Edge*. Philadelphia, PA: Temple University Press.

16. Parker, Laurence, and Marvin Lynn. 2002. "What's Race Got to Do with It? Critical Race Theory's Conflicts with and Connections to Qualititative Research Methodology and Epistomology." *Qualitative Inquiry* 8: 7–22.

17. Dvale, Steiner. 1996. *An Introduction to Qualitative Research Interviewing*. Thousand Oaks, CA: Sage Publications.

18. Feagin, Joe. R. 2007. Personal communication.

19. Weitzer, Ronald, and Steven A. Tuch. 2004. "Race and Perceptions of Police Misconduct." *Social Problems* 51: 305–25, pp. 313–15.

20. Shaw, Clifford. 1966. *The Jack-Roller: A Delinquent Boy's Own Story*. Chicago: University of Chicago Press.

21. Shaw, Clifford R., and Henry D. McKay. 1942. *Juvenile Delinquency and Urban Areas: A Study of Rates of Delinquents in Relation to Differential Characteristics of Local Communities in American Cities*. Chicago: University of Chicago Press.

22. Lanier, Mark M., and Stuart Henry. *Essential Criminology*.

23. Klockars, Carl B. 1974. *The Professional Fence*. New York: Free Press.

24. Frankenberg, Ruth. 1994. *White Women, Race Matters: The Social Construction of Whiteness*. New York: Routledge.

25. Bolton, Jr., Kenneth, and Joe R. Feagin. 2004. *Black in Blue: African-American Police Officers and Racism*. New York: Routledge, p. 31.

26. van den Hoonaard, Will C. 1997. *Working with Sensitizing Concepts: Analytical Field Research*. Thousand Oaks, CA: Sage Publications, p. 61.

27. Burawoy, Michael. 1991. "The Extended Case Method." Pp. 271–87 in *Ethnography Unbound: Power and Resistance in the Modern Metropolis,* Michael Burawoy, Alice Burton, Ann Arnett Ferguson, and Kathryn J. Fox, eds. Berkeley: University of California Press, p. 282.

28. Russell, Margaret M. 1992. "Entering Great America: Reflections on Race and the Convergence of Progressive Legal Theory and Practice. *Hastings Law Journal* 43: 749–67, p. 758.

29. Jamal, Samina, "Critical Ethnography," p. 235; Fine, Michelle. 2006. "Bearing Witness: Methods for Researching Repression and Resistance—A Textbook for Critical Research." *Social Justice Research* 19: 83–108.

30. Wahab, Amar. 2005. "Consuming Narratives: Questioning Authority and the Politics of Representation in Social Science Research." Pp. 29–51 in *Critical Issues in Anti-Racist Research Methodologies,* edited by George J. Sefa Dei and Gurpreet Singh Johal. New York: Peter Lang Publishing, pp. 32–33.

31. Rosaldo, Renato. 1999. "Cultural Citizenship, Inequality, and Multiculturalism." Pp. 253–61 in *Race, Identity, and Citizenship: A Reader,* Rodolfo D. Torres, Louis F. Miron, and Jonathan Xavier Inda, eds. Malden, MA: Blackwell Publishers, p. 260.

32. Bonilla-Silva, Eduardo. 2003. *Racism without Racists: Color-Blind Racism and the Persistence of Racial Inequality in the United States*. Lanham, MD: Rowman & Littlefield Publishers, p. 13; Fine, "Bearing Witness."

33. Tierney, William G., and Yvonna S. Lincoln, eds. 1997. *Representation and the Text: Re-Framing the Narrative Voice*. Albany: State University of New York Press, p. viii.

34. Strauss, Anselm, and Juliet Corbin. 1998. *Basics of Qualitative Research: Techniques and Procedures for Developing Grounded Theory*. Thousand Oaks, CA: Sage Publications, p. 13.

35. Bonilla-Silva, *Racism without Racists,* p. 13.

36. Omi, Michael, and Howard Winant. 1994. *Racial Formation in the United States from the 1960s to the 1990s*. New York: Routledge.

37. Omi and Winant, *Racial Formation in the United States from the 1960s to the 1990s,* p.10.

38. Bonilla-Silva, *Racism without Racists,* p. 196.

39. Omi and Winant, *Racial Formation in the United States from the 1960s to the 1990s,* p. vii.

40. Young, Alford. 2008. "White Ethnographers on the Experiences of African American Men: Then and Now." Pp. 179–200 in *White Logic, White Methods: Racism and Methodology,* Tukufu Zuberi and Eduardo Bonilla-Silva, eds. Lanham, MD: Rowman & Littlefield.

41. Twine, France Winddance, and Jonathan W. Warren. 2000. *Racing Research, Researching Race: Methodological Dilemmas in Critical Race Studies*. New York: New York University Press.

42. Barak, Flavin, and Leighton, *Class, Race, Gender, and Crime*; Lanier and Henry, *Essential Criminology*.

43. Russell, Katheryn K. 1998. *The Color of Crime: Racial Hoaxes, White Fear, Black Protectionism, Police Harassment, and Other Macroaggressions*. New York: New York University Press.

44. Zuberi, Tukufu, and Eduardo Bonilla-Silva. 2008. *White Logic, White Methods: Racism and Methodology*. Lanham, MD: Rowman & Littlefield, p. 338.

45. Feagin, Joe R. 2006. *Systemic Racism: A Theory of Oppression*. New York: Routledge, p. 2.

46. Feagin, *Systemic Racism*, p. 21.

47. Feagin, *Systemic Racism*, p. 25.

48. Collins, Patricia Hill. 2000. *Black Feminist Thought: Knowledge, Consciousness, and the Politics of Empowerment*. New York: Routledge.

49. Feagin, *Systemic Racism*, p. 33.

50. Russell, *The Color of Crime*.

51. Weitzer, Ronald, and Steven A. Tuch. 2006. *Race and Policing in America: Conflict and Reform*. Cambridge, UK: Cambridge University Press, p. 19.

52. Feagin, *Systemic Racism*, p. 277.

53. Bolton and Feagin, *Black in Blue*, p. 32.

54. Bolton and Feagin, *Black in Blue*, p. 32.

55. DuBois, W. E. B. 1986. *Writings: The Suppression of the Slave Trade; The Souls of Black Folks; Dusk of Dawn; Essays and Articles*. New York: Literary Classics of the United States-Library of America.

56. Foucault, *Discipline & Punish*.

57. Omi and Winant, *Racial Formation in the United States from the 1960s to the 1990s*.

58. Gabbidon, Shaun L., Helen Taylor Greene, and Vernetta D. Young, eds. 2002. *African American Classics in Criminology & Criminal Justice*. New York: Sage Publications.

59. DuBois, W. E. B., *Writing*, p. 364.

60. Foucault, *Discipline & Punish*, p. 201.

61. Foucault, *Discipline & Punish*, p. 101.

62. Bonilla-Silva, *Racism without Racists*.

63. Feagin, *Systemic Racism*.

64. Feagin, *Systemic Racism*, p. 31.

65. Collins, *Black Feminist Thought*.

66. Barak, Flavin, and Leighton, *Class, Race, Gender, and Crime*; Marchetti, Elena. 2008. "Intersectional Race and Gender Analyses: Why Legal Processes Just Don't Get It." *Social Legal Studies* 1: 155–74.

67. Barak, Flavin, and Leighton, *Class, Race, Gender, and Crime*.

68. Collins, *Black Feminist Thought*, p. 201.

69. Collins, *Black Feminist Thought*, p. 202.

70. Collins, *Black Feminist Thought*, p. 204.

71. West, Candace, and Sarah Fenstermaker. 1995. "Doing Difference." *Gender & Society* 9: 8–37.

72. Wilson, Bianca Della Marie, and Robin Lin Miller. 2002. "Strategies for Managing Heterosexism Used among African American Gay and Bisexual Men." *Journal of Black Psychology* 28: 371–91.

73. Collins, *Black Feminist Thought*, p. 203.
74. Collins, *Black Feminist Thought*, p. 221.
75. Yosso, Tara J., and David G. Garcia. 2007. "'This is No Slum!': A Critical Race Theory Analysis of Community Cultural Wealth in Culture Clash's Chavez Ravine." *Aztlan: A Journal of Chicano Studies* 32: 145–79.
76. Haenfler, Ross. 2004. "Rethinking Subcultural Resistance: Core Values of the Straight Edge Movement." *Journal of Contemporary Ethnography* 33: 406–36, p. 429.
77. Collins, *Black Feminist Thought*, p. 203.

5

Concepts in Citizenship

No country can grow and develop where there is no order, and a society without equal justice will self-destruct. There must be law and that law must be tempered by justice. And that justice must be for all!

Melvin P. Sikes[1]

I hope to reconfigure the lens of examination on perception-oriented racial profiling research. Personal and vicarious ("imagined participation") experiences are considered to be primary factors in explaining why individuals perceive a traffic stop as racialized. Critical orientations consider this inquiry as an effort to discount the everyday oppressions faced by people of color and asks instead, What does a racializing and criminalizing encounter with the state mean to the social actors who experience the phenomenon? The personal and vicarious focus in the mainstream research provides a useful framework for comparing traditional examinations of racial profiling with a critical race perspective. As noted in the closing of chapter 4, citizenship emerged as the dominant narrative in my interviews. Because the citizenship narrative is so represented in my respondents' reflections on racial profiling, I devote this brief chapter to consideration of it before going into the qualitative analysis in chapters 6 and 7.

Citizenship is reflected discursively by respondents' embracement of the liberty and justice framework of democratic ideals. Respondents directly and indirectly engage a citizens' rights discourse involving protections, rights, social contract obligations between the state and the citizenry, Americana, patriotism, and concern for the collective, among other issues. The citizenship construct (the invocation of the liberty and rights frame however embedded in the panopticon effect and double consciousness) is invoked in both the personal experience and vicarious experience explications. As such, both data chapters to follow incorporate citizenship as a main construct but, for analytical purposes, I focus on it in chapter 6 where I concentrate on the personal experience variable. Chapter 7 centers on the vicarious experience variable in the context of collective memory and the lesson.

Panopticonism, in the spirit of Foucault, centers on the sense of constant surveillance, monitoring, and patrolling that many of the respondents experience in their everyday relations with the state. I am concerned with the regularity of state intervention via the traffic stop and respondents' linkages of panopticonism to a denial of citizenship. For example, one respondent comments that getting stopped by the police on occasion is part of "the black experience." Similarly, DuBois's double consciousness, that great divide experienced by people of color in their engagements of substantive citizenship, is a constant in both data chapters. Chapter 6 is also where I offer analysis of resistance to oppression, an issue I briefly engage at the conclusion of this chapter.

With the vicarious experience factor, examined in chapter 7, I reject the white logic premise evident in the current literature that suggests people of color amplify one another's experiences with law enforcement and create their own problems with the state by fanning the flames in their discussions of law enforcement. The dominant narratives that emerge contextualize others' experiences with the racial state within a collective memory framework (more specifically "the lesson") that has long been used as a way for oppressed communities to negotiate the racial terrain in the United States. These themes are critical to understanding racial domination by the state.

What is it about the traffic stop encounter that creates a racialized experience for communities of color? I hope to complicate the current literature's answer that perceptions—often contrasted to *reality* in the mainstream literature as my analysis will demonstrate—explain the phenomenon in a meaningful way. For many people of color, the *racialized* traffic stop is an everyday reminder of a much broader system of racial inequality in society than the mere traffic stop—from a white racial frame[2] and white logic[3] perspective—would suggest. The white gaze that situates the racial profiling research, for example, may consider the traffic stop a mere inconvenience or suggest that if the motorist is not guilty of any crime, why should he contest the situation? Another frequent argument made in pro-profiling debates, as discussed earlier, is the line of reasoning referred to as *rational discrimination* that looks to the hue of the criminal justice system to justify targeted law enforcement of people of color. Contrary to current literature assumptions, the effect of what is experienced to be a racialized encounter with law enforcement is not limited to the police–minority relationship. Data from my respondents point to a break from citizenship during and following these encounters. The encounters are often considered watershed moments in the lives of people of color that alter their relationship with the state, a relationship already tenuous given the historical and contemporary practices of the state.

CITIZENSHIP

In the two chapters to follow, respondents reflect upon deep levels of alienation, distrust, and righteous anger that they experience following a racialized encounter with the state. Citizenship concerns and expectations emerge in subtle and direct ways throughout many of the interviews. I begin this section by discussing at some length the various conceptions of citizenship and the various ways citizenship marks the police–minority relationship.

Blacks and other people of color are often the most ardent defenders of the rights extended to Americans discursively in the liberty and justice rights framework that characterizes the citizenship realm.[4] Although these rights are extended substantively for whites, they are not extended substantively for many people of color. As a consequence, people of color assess critically the rights ideology as it operates in practice and reject the white racial frame that positions the rights discourse as mere, yet effective, rhetoric. They uphold the promise of equal protection under the law but recognize that that pledge is rooted in a system of racial enforcement of the law. In sum, people of color engage the liberty and justice frame discursively primarily to address its limitations in practice (an issue of walking the talk) while whites generally engage similar frames only rhetorically, that is, not to point out contradictions in how the system works in practice but to point to the *ideals* of the system that work in their experience. White racial frame orientations work to prevent whites from seriously dissecting the fracture between founding constitutional ideals—the issue of true extension of citizenship—and how things operate on the street.

VARIOUS CONCEPTIONS OF CITIZENSHIP

For Aristotle, a citizen is one who rules and is ruled in turn. *Citizenship* is characterized by inclusion and exclusion, by formal and informal means that either promote or deny "full social, economic, and political rights."[5] A well-cited definition of citizenship is that it is concerned with the rule of law and its application to the liberty of individuals and their right to justice.[6] A primary right of the citizen is freedom from state intervention, unless, for example, there exists probable cause as articulated by the Fourth Amendment to the U.S. Constitution. Citizenship is marked discursively by the liberty and justice rights framework that is embraced as a standard of democratic ideals. Yet as is evident in the current analysis, the liberty and justice framework also serves as a ruling ideology posited by dominant whites to bolster the white racial frame that organizes society. The white racial frame is dependent on the ideals of liberty and justice as these ideals help explain (to whites, primarily) the dominant position of whites in society as well as the subordinate position of communities of color in society. Bonilla-Silva characterizes whites' ability to engage similar discourses as *abstract liberal* thinking in which the racial ordering in the United States is viewed as emerging from, for example, an individualistic "follow the rules, work hard" mentality.[7] This perspective allows whites (and some people of color) to ignore social structural restraints deeply embedded in the normal operations of society in their explanations of the racial order.

The narrowing of the "constitutional grant of citizenship" manifests in both overt and covert ways over the course of United States' history.[8] From Richard Delgado's critical race theory perspective, the law constructs a racialized citizen. The Constitution itself was written by slaveholding white males who intended for the protections of liberty and justice to be extended only to those who mirrored their own image, namely, white male property owners who comprised roughly 20 percent of the population. Later, literacy tests and national origin quotas characterized more obvious maneuvers, though denial of substantive citizenship is continuous through to the current era of color-blind racism. Racial profiling is one of the more subtle ways that racial oppression via denial of citizenship operates in the current era.

Citizenship may also involve "a transcendence, a greater collectivity in which we get beyond our local identities and concerns."[9] This aspect of citizenship is evident in the recurrent notions of "this problem is bigger than me and my experience with it" comments from my respondents. T. McLaughlin[10] characterizes citizenship from a *minimalist* view that is formal and legal and from a *maximalist* standpoint that incorporates broader recognition of collectivity and democratic ideals, while Patricia Williams[11] describes the context of citizenship in the following:

> If one looks at documents like the Declaration of Independence and the Constitution, one can see how they marry aspects of consent and aspects

> of symbology—for example, concepts like the notion of freedom. On the one hand there is the letter of the law exalted in these documents, which describes a specific range of rights and precepts. On the other hand there is the spirit of the law, the symbology of freedom, which is in some ways utterly meaningless or empty—although at the same time the very emptiness provides a vessel to be filled with possibility, with a plurality of autonomous yearnings.

As well, citizenship has implicit notions of sameness and collectivity that does not address multicultural, multiconcern issues that emerge in a stratified state. Attempts at transcending personal concerns for the good of the collective subjugates oppressed groups because their concerns are likely not at the fore of the collective.[12] Theoretically, engaging in the discourse and activity of "transcendent" citizenship reinforces white privilege. As Kathleen Jones states:[13]

> a citizen is one whose membership is contingent upon the ultimate subordination of the specific bonds of gender, race, and class—indeed, all particularized identities—in favor, most often, of a national identity and loyalty to the state. To become a citizen is to trade one's particular identity for an abstract, public self. But the identification of citizens and the definition of citizenship is derived from the representation of the behavior of a group with particular race, gender, and class characteristics (white male elites) as the model of citizenship for all individuals.

In this excerpt, Jones comments on citizenship's "ultimate subordination" of "particularized identities" in favor of a greater bond to the nation. A similar discourse is found in discussion of the law more generally when it is presented as being a primarily neutral form of social control not influenced by systems of power and by which everyone should abide. In these more critical examinations of citizenship, whiteness is an incorporated quality of citizenship in the United States. While people of color may be formally extended citizenship, its inherent protections are not extended.[14]

Another fundamental component of citizenship is the reciprocity that it implies between the state and its citizenry. This concept, the contractual way of viewing citizenship, posits that the state and the citizenry have certain rights and obligations that bind each other.[15] The citizen has rights to a certain degree of autonomy and protections in exchange for following guidelines of behavior that do not undermine the state's supreme authority. The social contract framework suggests an agreement between entities to do *something* and is specifically a "theory that founds government on the popular consent of individuals taken as equals."[16] Charles Mills describes how the contract is an effort to develop "a trust of rights and powers" in a relationship with a governing entity. When racialization occurs, Mills argues that the social contract central to Western political theory becomes "not a contract between everybody ('we the people'), but between just the people who count, the people who really are people ('we the white people'). So it is a Racial Contract."[17]

Racial profiling is facilitated by a negation of the citizenship's ability to demand state accountability. People of color may be viewed as nonparticipatory in the other realms of civic life—the political realm, for instance (realistically due to disenchantment with the system and disenfranchisement in the system)—thus officers may view themselves as not as accountable to and not *as* accountable for in their actions. Citizenship also concerns spatial governance—the *who belongs where* reality that regulates the racial state. However, the out-of-place doctrine that frames the police–minority relationship is not only about the physical boundaries that are racialized in the United States. As indicated by my respondents, expressing knowledge of rights and civil protections during an encounter with law enforcement sometimes leads to escalated "anti-citizen" reactions from the police. People of color in these encounters are viewed as not knowing *their place* when they invoke the citizenship realm. I note here that black and Latino respondents reflect in similar ways on the impact of racial profiling in their lives, thus pointing to the largely white-bounded nature of citizenship in practice in the United States and the common alliances that the white racial frame invokes.

DUBOIS AND DOUBLE CONSCIOUSNESS

DuBois's notion of *double consciousness* is one of the primary theoretical frames concerning citizenship that emerge in the analysis to follow. As discussed earlier in this book, double consciousness is DuBois's concern with reconciling the experience of being black (more generally, a person of color) with the experience of being a full citizen and receiving all the rights that go with equal protection under the law. Likely one of the most cited quotes in race studies, DuBois described the sense of double consciousness in this way: "One ever feels his two-ness,—an American, a Negro; two souls, two thoughts, two unreconciled strivings; two warring ideals in one dark body, whose dogged strength alone keeps it from being torn asunder."[18] The sense of "two-ness" described by DuBois is a direct reference to the limits of citizenship in practice for people of color when they confront, with varying modes of resistance, the social fact of racialized citizenship emergent through social control processes of the state.

Double consciousness, in the following analysis, is evident when respondents acknowledge the impact of racial status on their encounters with the state, thus countering the contemporary (white) public notion that the state operates in a color-blind manner. Double consciousness is a useful framework when examining these accounts of personal experience with law enforcement as the concept is reflective of larger racial forces that shape our political landscape and not limited to the brevity of the traffic stop itself that is the focus of the current racial profiling literature. References to the liberty and justice frame, discussed above, are a complex discourse that shapes conceptions of citizenship yet centers on the *anti*-citizen experiences they are subjected to in practice.

More than a century after DuBois's scholarship on double consciousness, the situation, though clouded by white-framed claims of racial progress, remains formidable. The forms of racial oppression may have changed, especially in the post-Civil Rights era with its color-blind racism pursuits, but the underlying maintenance of the racial status quo remains. This is evident in a quote from one of my respondents that people of color, when they encounter racialization and criminalization processes from the state, "didn't have a picture that we would get treated like that in today's society."

Respondents in the following analysis offer rich accounts of criminalizing encounters with law enforcement, indicating the degree to which they have been marked by the encounter. As discussed earlier, these narratives include a lack of protection from the state, struggles when invoking their own knowledge of rights, lack of accountability from the state, and a sense of the collective identity that manifests as personal troubles being politically constituted. The ideology is characterized in part by freedom from unwarranted state intervention typified in racialized surveillance practices of the state. For example, one respondent comments that individuals "belong" in the United States when they get treated fairly under the Constitution. This discourse is posited as a counter to the white racist frame that allows whites to engage similar ideas to explain the social order as race neutral.[19] These sometimes painfully detailed stories, however, are most disturbing because of the aftereffects of the encounters—the connections made to broader oppressions underpinning the legal realm.

PROCEDURAL JUSTICE FRAMEWORK

Although the thrust of my critique of the current literature stems from its lack of focus on citizenship with an issue that is decidedly about *citizenship*, I view Tom Tyler and Cheryl Wakslak's[20] work on procedural justice as an important step in recognizing the link between the discursive and practical implications of the justice and liberty rights frame.

In the rare instances when the racial profiling literature does address citizenship in general terms, it comes in the muted form of the procedural justice framework put forth most notably by Tyler and Wakslak.[21] Procedural justice concerns the treatment a citizen experiences during an encounter with law enforcement and whether the treatment is viewed as fair by the citizen. Researchers interested in procedural justice inquire about the quality of decision making and treatment by law enforcement and about evaluations of trustworthiness of the police during a given encounter. The procedural justice framework assumed a primary spot in the second wave of research on racial profiling that focused on what makes an individual perceive he is being racially profiled. According to this framework, individuals who are treated courteously, informed of their rights, and told why the police are taking certain actions during an encounter are less likely to consider the encounter in the racial profiling realm.[22]

The racial profiling literature, however, is limited in extending the procedural justice concept beyond the brevity of the traffic stop. The fair treatment aspect of the procedural justice framework is generally bounded within the specific police–citizen encounter. I argue that while the procedural justice framework is useful to an extent, its focus on the micro-level is limiting.

The respondents in the following analysis make clear that not only does an encounter with the police that falls short of procedural justice ideals influence their view of the police generally, they establish linkages between the micro-level traffic stop and citizenship at the broader societal level because the traffic stop is representative of larger social forces of racial oppression that manifest in the ordinary. Communities of color situate their personal experiences into broader frames of reference that are reflected in Collins's concept that personal troubles are politically constituted.[23]

Panopticonism emerges discursively in the citizenship liberty and rights frame engaged by the respondents because a mainstay of citizenship and social contract obligations is a level of autonomy from state intervention. The use of citizenship discourse reflects the respondents' own position that they are due the rights and protections of citizenship and thus resist the subordinate identity imposed by the state via hyper-surveillance. A guiding question of the current examination of racial profiling is what are the mechanisms that emerge to contextualize and resist racial oppression in the form of racial profiling? This issue of resistance is the issue I turn to in chapter 6.

CONCLUSION

The negative criminalizing identity imposed upon many people of color is clearly rejected in the dominant narratives that accompany the citizenship discourse. As described in an analysis of David Walker's nineteenth-century *Appeal to the Colored Citizens of the World*, faith in the ideology of citizenship and democracy does not prevent communities of color from condemning the practices of the state.[24] Respondents' engagement of citizenship discourse reflects their own possession of citizenship that takes priority over the subordinate identity imposed by the state. They occupy a regulatory position on citizen–state relations by remaining tied to the dominant frames of citizenship and democracy. Their lived experiences demonstrate the limits of citizenship placed upon them by the state yet they still uphold the "liberty and justice" rights framework that has guided direct and indirect forms of resistance against racial oppression for centuries. Respondents show that the ideal of citizenship can hold up as an ideology—demonstrated by their engagement of the citizenship discourse and the identity they ultimately contextualize themselves within—while the state's obligation to citizenship is unfulfilled.

Accompanying the narratives on citizenship are accounts of the various modes of resistance that emerge in the wake of racialized and criminalized encounters with the state. For DuBois, the awareness of both worlds—here, the world of citizen and the world of "second-class" citizen—is clearly racialized. Yet, awareness of the oppression is not entirely burdensome because of the critical consciousness and resistance to domination borne from the experience. The analysis that follows in chapters 6 and 7 flows in and out of the various dimensions of citizenship and resistance to state practices that deny citizenship. As is the case with the dominant narrative of citizenship, none of the existing literature on racial profiling examines the dominant narrative of resistance. In the following chapters, my hope is to privilege the voices of historically silenced people of color and contextualize their experiences within critical race and social control frameworks so that their legitimate knowledge of the social phenomenon of racialized law enforcement is heard, and heard loudly.

NOTES

1. Sikes, Melvin P. 1975. *The Administration of Injustice*. New York: Harper & Row Publishers.
2. Feagin, Joe R. 2006. *Systemic Racism: A Theory of Oppression*. New York: Routledge.

3. Bonilla-Silva, Eduardo. 2003. *Racism without Racists: Color-Blind Racism and the Persistence of Racial Inequality in the United States*. Lanham, MD: Rowman & Littlefield.
4. Feagin, *Systemic Racism*.
5. Cook, Dee. 1999. "Racism, Citizenship and Exclusion." Pp. 136–57 in *Racism & Criminology*, Dee Cook and Barbara Hudson, eds. London: Sage Publications, p. 136.
6. Marshall, Thomas Humphrey. 1964. *Class, Citizenship, and Social Development: Essays*. Garden City, NY: Doubleday.
7. Bonilla-Silva, *Racism without Racists*.
8. Delgado, Richard. 1999. "Citizenship." Pp. 247–52 in *Race, Identity, and Citizenship: A Reader*, Rodolfo D. Torres, Louis F. Miron, and Jonathan Xavier Inda, eds. Malden, MA: Blackwell Publishers, p. 248.
9. Phillips, Anne. 1993. *Democracy and Difference*. University Park: Pennsylvania State University Press, p. 81.
10. McLaughlin, T. 1992. "Citizenship, Diversity and Education: A Philosophical Perspective." *Journal of Moral Education* 21: 235–51.
11. Williams, Patricia J. 1991. *The Alchemy of Race and Rights*. Cambridge, MA: Harvard University Press, p. 16.
12. Young, Iris Marion. 1989. "Polity and Group Difference: A Critique of the Ideal of Universal Citizenship." *Ethics* 99: 250–74.
13. Jones, Kathleen B. 1990. "Citizenship in a Woman-Friendly Polity." *Signs* 15: 781–812, p. 784.
14. Cook, "Racism, Citizenship and Exclusion."
15. Kerber, Linda K. 1998. *No Constitutional Right to Be Ladies: Women and the Obligations of Citizenship*. New York: Hill and Wang.
16. Mills, Charles W. 1997. *The Racial Contract*. Ithaca, NY: Cornell University Press, p. 3.
17. Mills, *The Racial Contract*, p. 3.
18. DuBois, W. E. B. 1986. *Writings: The Suppression of the Slave Trade; The Souls of Black Folks; Dusk of Dawn; Essays and Articles*. New York: Literary Classics of the United States-Library of America, p. 364.
19. Feagin, *Systemic Racism*.
20. Tyler, Tom, and Cheryl J. Wakslak. 2004. "Profiling and Police Legitimacy: Procedural Justice, Attributions of Motive, and Acceptance of Police Authority." *Criminology* 42: 253–82.
21. Tyler Wakslak, "Profiling and Police Legitimacy."
22. Weitzer, Ronald, and Steven A. Tuch. 2006. *Race and Policing in America: Conflict and Reform*. Cambridge, UK: Cambridge University Press.
23. Collins, Patricia Hill. 2000. *Black Feminist Thought: Knowledge, Consciousness, and the Politics of Empowerment*. New York: Routledge.
24. Walker, David. 2000. *David Walker's Appeal to the Coloured Citizens of the World*, edited by Peter P. Hinks. University Park: Pennsylvania State University.

III

6

An Ethnographic Reading on Racial Profiling

My specific goal in this chapter is to offer examples of interview data that demonstrate the salience of citizenship and resistance to racial oppression to give meaning to the current literature's concern with *personal experience* with law enforcement. The narratives below are from fifteen of the twenty-six overall respondents in my study.[1] After the first few interviews, it became clear to me that the theme of citizenship and resistance to racializing and criminalizing processes of the state were emerging as dominant narratives. Qualitative research analysis involves the revelation of dominant narratives from interview data: The narratives analyzed in this chapter were chosen because they were particularly illuminating in articulation of the issues of concern. I learned from my respondents that anti-citizenship practices by the state toward people of color, in many instances, provoke stronger commitment to the ideals of the liberty and civil rights, in addition to provoking both direct and indirect protests to the regularity of these practices.

FIFTEEN REFLECTIVE LAW ENFORCEMENT–CITIZEN ENCOUNTERS

Darrell, a black male in his twenties with some college, describes how an awareness of citizenship issues influenced his only arrest encounter (for a very minor infraction) with law enforcement. In the excerpt below, I asked Darrell if he could offer any examples where race was a factor in his encounters with law enforcement.

YYYYEEEEPPP! When I was 18, a few months out of high school, I was arrested for my first and last time. In short it was just, basically the officer involved didn't like my mouth or the fact that I was a young black male out doing what I was doing—which wasn't illegal. But more so, he didn't like the fact that I knew the laws. My mother had taught me. She did citizen's police academy. I used to read her books. I was abreast of what extent I could go to as far as when a law enforcement officer stops you—whether on foot or in a vehicle. I was singled out basically for no reason. Like I said, partly because of my mouth but for no reason at all. After the arrest came down and I was booked and everything, I got in the holding cell. When they fingerprinted me and took my snapshots, I was subjected to being called . . . racial slurs, racial epithets. Just a lot of things. They figured that, this was just my opinion, because of my mouth and because of the knowledge I had. Me being aware as I was at that age. Perhaps they would break me or. . . . I don't know. They did what they did.

In this excerpt, Darrell frames himself as knowledgeable about the law in part because of his mother's involvement with the community police academy. He is aware that his knowledge of the law, as well as his minority racial status and youthfulness, were factors that led to the officers communicating that he did *not know his place.* This points to the various modes that the *out-of-place doctrine* can come in—it is not restricted to social control of spatial ground but, as expressed here, also applies to how expressing one's knowledge of rights may signal to the racial state that one is outside of domains the state deems (racially) appropriate. Speaking in a measured tone, Darrell remarks that the handling he received in the police department involved racial slurs and epithets. I noted during the interview that he did not linger over this statement of fact or express surprise about the language used by the law enforcement officers. This may reflect a regularity of experience with degradation ceremonies for young men of color, of which the racial profiling traffic stop is a mainstay. Significantly, Darrell remarks that the officers intended to "break" him, a reference to the days of slavery and the *breaking* of willful slaves (those who expressed resistance to oppression). As discussed by Russell[2] in her discussion of how slave codes, black codes, Jim Crow, and other racialized law *continuously* facilitates (though in varying degrees of formality) the racial order in the United States into contemporary times, and evident from Darrell's alignment of his contemporary experiences with practices during slavery, the historically bounded issue of slavery may be invoked as analogous to how the state operates in a racialized way contemporarily.

A common theme for Darrell involves his knowledge of the rights and protections that fall under the citizenship ideal:

I have that right to say what I need to say in order to defend myself. To make him [an officer] aware that I know what I'm talking about and that I know

> what the laws are. To let him know that I'm not going to just sit up here and let him do what he's doing without knowing that I'm aware that he's doing it to me.

Resistance emerges here in the form of a rejection of white authority and power and an assumption of the rights of citizenship as a person of color. Darrell also self-defines the situation and makes clear that the awareness of racial oppression in itself is a form of opposition to it. Both Darrell and his mother engage in resistance to racial oppression by making tangible, political changes in their lives by becoming educated about the institution of law enforcement. The insight contained in DuBois's double consciousness is evident: Darrell identifies as a citizen and clearly understands protections due under full citizenship, while recognizing the limitations he is subjected to as a young man of color.

Another respondent, Javier, a Latino in his late teens with some college education, contrasts his lived experiences with the experiences of whites in similar situations with law enforcement.

> I had gotten an MIP (minor in possession). Me and four of my friends . . . it was kind of late and it was dark out. We were parked near the shore. We had Budweiser on us and we were drinking. We obviously got stopped. After we got the tickets and everything, we had stayed there. Of course we had to spill out all of the beers. We went walking down the beach and there were a couple of people . . . they were white. They had a bonfire and all that. They had like a little party. We asked them—"did the cops stop by here?" They said "yeah." I noticed that some of them didn't look too old. They said they didn't even get questioned or anything. I was pretty mad about that. I thought that these cops—I thought it was some kind of a racial thing. I mean it was clear over here in my little junkie car, we don't have a fire or lights or anything and it is only four of us. Then, the other people have the big bonfire and everything out and had a big radio making lots of noise. I was thinking why didn't they get stopped? Isn't that more of probable cause?

Javier's sense is that his experience was criminalizing through the actions of the state when similar actions by a group of young white males were not criminalized. A fundamental component of racial profiling is the targeted application of law enforcement resources to communities of color when whites engage in similar behaviors but do not receive similar scrutiny. Javier's urgency in contrasting his experience with the group of white youths points to his awareness that the rule of law theoretically inherent to the citizen–state relationship is differentially imposed. It provides a scenario of how people of color do not necessarily make immediate assumptions about racialization processes in society (the white logic concept of playing the race card) but instead consider contextualizing factors to explain social phenomenon. Javier directly engages citizenship discourse through his use of the expression "probable cause"—a significant and formal legal element of citizen protections against state intervention, thus constructing a constitutionally bounded sense of identity for himself. Per Collins's conceptualization, this is resistance in the form of the rejection of whiteness equaling authority and truth.[3]

Kimberly, a black female in her thirties earning a graduate degree, relays one memorable encounter with the police in which, based on citizenship expectations, she questioned the treatment she received from law enforcement.

> I was pulled over by a police officer and I wasn't really sure why. It's not like I was driving a flashy car—I was driving a Volkswagen Fox. Once the police came behind me, it was daytime so I thought I was safe and I pulled over. Immediately when the police officer came up, the first question that he asked me—"I want to ask you, do you have any drugs or weapons in your car?" I was so shocked that he asked me that. I looked at him and I said "Why are you asking me that?" He said "Ma'am, I'm asking the questions here. Do you have any drugs or weapons in your car?" I said "Now wait a minute. I want to know if this is standard policy to ask this question or is this a question that you are asking me because I'm a black, you know, black person driving?" At that particular time he told me "Ma'am, step out of the car." At this point, I'm not sure who I'm dealing with—this white officer and he's asking me this question. I'm somewhat defensive. He proceeded to let me know that he didn't appreciate me letting him know that he wasn't being objective in doing, performing his job. Again, I still want to know! Is this standard procedure or do you ask everybody? He completely ignored me and went around the car looking for stuff on my car.

Kimberly's narrative touches on a number of concerns salient to police–minority relations. First, she makes a connection between the type of vehicle she drives and the likelihood of getting stopped by the police. In the police–minority relations literature, the vehicle emerges as context for officer decision making.[4] "Flashy" cars may signal potential drug dealing. The connotation is that motorists of color cannot afford expensive cars unless they are involved in the drug trade. Kimberly remarks that the setting of daylight offered her a sense of safety, thus suggesting that a traffic stop in the cover of night is a concern for her—likely due to her status as both a female and a person of color. Her outrage over the incident is provoked by the criminalization, and the immediacy of the criminalization, that occurs with the officer's initial question if she has drugs or weapons in her possession. Kimberly invokes the citizenship realm by asking the officer about "standard policy" procedures that are theoretically established to provide a uniform experience for citizens in their encounters with law enforcement. Resisting the ideology of whiteness-equals-authority, she directly inserts the issue of race into the encounter, on her own terms, by inquiring if her racial status was the motivation for the traffic stop. Assertion of citizenship prompts the officer to increase his level of coercion and authority over Kimberly as he dismisses her questioning of his neutrality. Kimberly continues to assert her citizenship, pointedly telling the nonresponsive officer: "I still want to know!" Noticeably upset at this point in the interview, Kimberly left me with the impression that the encounter was recent given the vivid and rawness of her memory. Later she reveals that the event occurred some fifteen years prior, thus indicating the staying power of these watershed events and their ability, for some, to provoke resistance. In Kimberly's case, for example, she eventually started a nonprofit community organization and returned to school to pursue a doctorate—clearly political, tangible instances of creating change in her life and the lives of others. Kimberly concludes the narrative with remarks on how the increased coercion from the officer led to additional resistance on her part.

> He let me know that he was going to note my attitude on the ticket. I was like—"OK, great . . . Sergeant . . . Officer. . . ." I looked at his name tag. "I'm going to note your attitude as well because you still haven't answered my question." At that point, he became defensive and was telling me that he could actually, because of a light, leave my car on the side of the road and [I would need to] walk wherever I needed to go. I said "Now look, there might be a lot of things that you can do but one thing that I won't do when I leave this particular point—I will not be walking! If that means you have to give me a ride where I need to go."
>
> He didn't give me a citation [for speeding]. I sat there. It was strange to me. More and more since I didn't get the citation I realized that, or I felt that, it was strictly an issue of race. I didn't even know why he pulled me over. Initially, it's not that I was speeding. I didn't know what that was about. I did eventually call into the station and I asked if that was a standard question. I was told that if the officer felt like that was something—I guess in the context then that was a question that would be asked. I didn't think there was —anything about me that would give off the impression that I had drugs or weapons in my car. Even now, just talking about it . . . just evokes this passion or something within me that is like—wow, this did happen to me.

Kimberly has a direct confrontation with institutional power when she tells the officer that she has the authority to document the racialized way he is representing the state. The exchange also places Kimberly firmly in the citizenship realm as she invokes her rights to hold the state accountable for its actions. Following the officer's reassertion of authority and escalated coercion, including a threat to leave Kimberly on the side of the road, she acknowledges the power of the state in law enforcement encounters ("there might be a lot of things you can do . . .") but rejects the overreach of the law that the officer is describing. She is clearly self-defining the situation and rejecting the whiteness as authority construct by telling the officer what will be taking place.

In the second part of this excerpt, placing herself firmly in the citizen mode, Kimberly goes through formal channels to better understand the nature of the stop that obviously affected her deeply. Her eventual inquiry about standard policy to supervisors in the department is a direct call to the equal treatment under the law mantra of citizenship. Self-reflecting, Kimberly remarks that there wasn't "anything about me" that would signal illegal activity. Finally, she expresses some amount of surprise that the incident occurred and is struck by the level of emotion recalling the incident conjures up in her. Accountability, a primary component of the citizen–state ideal, is a major concern for many of the respondents. As discussed in earlier chapters, in the dominant narratives, accountability emerges in various ways, including direct calls to hold the state accountable to more subtle struggles to reconcile the citizenship ideology with experiential knowledge.

Another respondent gave an account of a humiliating and physical encounter with the police, occurring in front of his new bride, that also goes to the issue of state accountability. After a lengthy encounter with a Latino officer and his white partner, Carlos, a Latino in his thirties with a graduate degree, did not receive a ticket.

> He does not give me a ticket. I lose it. I demand a ticket. I want a ticket with his name, his badge number. I want all of that. He gets in his car and starts writing some things and takes off. I'm left there with who was he? I was so upset. . . . I wanted a ticket. He wouldn't give it to me. I was willing to pay $80 or $100 to get his name and badge number. But he wouldn't give me that justification.

Carlos has a direct confrontation with institutional authority of the police. He demands a ticket after the traffic stop quickly deteriorated following one of the officers' homophobic remarks when Carlos's wife confused pronouns when referring to her new husband (she was a recent immigrant whose first language was Spanish). Comments from Carlos that follow bring up another element of the traffic stop event that is likely only evident through a qualitative research approach. Not receiving formal documentation of wrongdoing following a traffic stop may *support* the view of people of color that the stop was unwarranted.[5] Citizenship theoretically entails protections against unwarranted governmental intrusion. People of color who are unduly interrupted in their daily affairs through criminalization processes like racial profiling may call for official notification of the intervention as a way to mark the individual officer's record—an issue of accountability from the state and resistance. The absence of official documentation of a traffic violation signals to the motorist of color that earlier suspicions that the stop was racially motivated are substantiated. The traffic stop, innocuous as it appears to some and especially when no citation is issued, is a micro-level occurrence that demonstrates the state's reach on a macro-level. Later, Carlos describes himself as a "changed man" because of the incident.

In the excerpt below, Carlos describes an array of identity concerns that emerge in the wake of a racialized traffic stop.

> It upsets me because you know as a veteran and a college student and whatever I think I am, um, that someone could look at me and the way I'm driving or the way I'm dressed and instigate a situation by pulling me over and stopping me from what I'm doing. I consider myself busy and with a purpose. I'm stopped for no apparent reason and not given a ticket. It does upset me. I know what they're looking for. . . . I know what they want and I am not that person. Yet, when they profile me, they think I fit this mold. I will pull him over and I will find something. It gets very upsetting because it's harassment. That's what it is. If you've never been in that situation, then you don't know what it feels like. And if you're not angry about it, it's because you've never been in that situation. This repeated situation.

Carlos engages in credentialing—making note of the various identities he holds—to position himself as someone who is showing commitment to society and holding up the ideals of citizenship, for example, through his veteran status and level of education. The noncitizen identity thrust upon him because of his ethnic status is difficult to reconcile to his own self-identification and points to the *two-ness* theorized by DuBois. The criminal identity imposed by the state via racial profiling is rejected ("I know what they want and I am not that person"), yet the toll of being criminalized is not denied. His narrative points to the experiential quality of racial oppression—the everydayness—and how the experience provokes resistance ("if you're not angry about it, it's because you've never been in that situation").

Carlos's account is unique because the main officer in the narrative is not white but a coethnic. There is some research on police culture suggesting officers of color may also engage in racial stereotyping once acculturated to institutional norms. Another respondent, Diana, a Latina in her thirties with some college, relayed an encounter with a white officer who she describes as treating her poorly. I asked Diana if the negative encounter shaped her general relations with law enforcement.

> I don't think it is an isolated issue because this guy was just, he was just serious. I think that over the years, I've ran into several cops in my life and I have met some real jerks—some real horror stories. Then there are some nice cops, really nice cops. I've even had an Hispanic cop treat my Hispanic sister like crap. I mean so horrible like—you're just a woman, we don't care if you are

> having marital problems, we don't care. I mean that's the attitude he gave her. I think about them doing it to their own people. I don't know if they just think they're . . . just because they are cops they can get away with it.

These examples point to the strong influence of the white racial frame (and male solidarity as well) on all members of American society, even people of color.[6]

Carlos's remarks on the issue are informative as he contextualizes it within the broader realm of white supremacy.

> He also was showing off. He was demeaning. I felt this Mexican man was demeaning me in front of this white man. That's exactly what it felt like. It made the situation so much more embarrassing. I have enough battles with white males and authority figures that I don't need someone who looks like me with a dumb country accent . . . with my last name . . . to belittle me.

Another indication of resistance in Carlos's narrative comes with his attempts to make tangible, political changes in his life following the encounter:

> When I got back, I went on-line and found information about MALDEF and ACLU. I didn't do anything but I got educated. So I felt empowered. The more educated I become, the more empowered I become. I demand you give me a ticket when you pull me over. I do make comments and they're not nice. I have made comments like "Are you pulling over white people today or is it just Mexicans?"

In this excerpt, Carlos not only indicates he has made tangible, political changes in his life, but also offers direct resistance to the state by demanding a ticket and throws off the white supremacy ideology by inserting the issue of ethnic status into his encounters with the state.

Jesse, a Latino in his early twenties with some college education, provides another example of how the instance of not receiving a ticket may be viewed as evidence that the traffic stop is race based. In the exchange below, he also invokes the "out-of-place" doctrine by acknowledging that there are certain social spaces where his freedom as a citizen is limited.

> J: I've been, all over this city, pulled over. I've kept count too—I know where not to drive. I've been pulled over eight times and I've only been given a ticket that one time. I already know the routine. They pull me over, they grab my license, I guess they run my license for warrants, and they just let me on my way. It's pretty blatant.
>
> K: So you're not ticketed for anything—they're not saying you're speeding?
>
> J: No, I'm not ticketed at all.

K: So this happened about eight times over the course of . . .

J: One year. I've only been here a year. I haven't even been here an entire year.

The experience of not receiving official documentation of an offense worthy of being pulled over is significant for Jesse and others who adhere to the idea that if they have not committed a meaningful enough infraction to be ticketed, why have they been subject to intervention by the state?

Edgar, a Latino in his twenties with a bachelor's degree, discusses the explicit nature of criminalization found in racial profiling processes. An underlying assumption framing the comments below is that there is an expected, theoretical neutrality of the state—a mainstay of citizenship—to which Edgar's experience is contrasted.

> I guess the worst thing about racial profiling when it comes to law enforcement is the fact you hear them actually—they admit it. That "we do."' "We are looking for Hispanic males driving this type of car . . . driving a nice car." They just flat out admit it. I took a course at [the university] and we did see several videotapes that were fairly recent and the cops themselves admitting it on tape. Their name there, badge number—it was almost like it was accepted. That it was an unspoken thing that without doubt we do racial profiling. It's pretty disconcerting. I'd even say I felt it a couple of times. If you've never felt it before, you don't know what it feels like. For me, the first time it was almost like, I was confused. I'm like, man . . . is what happened . . . did what happen just happen? It was one of those things that, you know, this has never happened to me before. It happened a second time and I kind of realized it. Wow, this is pretty messed up.
>
> You get that tense feeling. . . . That's not the way it should be. We should be able to look at them like they are my friendly neighborhood cop, you know, or Officer Friendly.

Edgar expresses initial disbelief about the overt way criminalization of communities of color may occur. As a young male in his twenties, the comments suggest his likely exposure to color-blind racism and the coded discourse that characterizes this contemporary manifestation of racism. Yet he clearly points to the experiential quality ("If you've never felt it before . . .") of racial profiling. The struggle with reconciling his underlying belief in citizenship with what he has come to experience himself is evident. Edgar has a sense of how his relationship with the police is theorized to operate, yet understands the relationship is different in practice, thus exhibiting the *double-consciousness* experience of many people of color.

One construct of citizenship is the contractual agreement that citizens give up some portion of their freedom in exchange for some facets of state protection. In the following, Edgar offers insight into how relations with the police affect the theoretical reciprocity among citizens and the state. Edgar explains the basic disconnect from the citizen–state contract that he and others experience as a result of negative relations. Because the social contract operates as a trust of rights and powers,[7] when it is broken through racialization and criminalization processes like racial profiling, nonstate actors experience disenfranchisement.

> I see it also as a betrayal. We as citizens put our faith in to people like that . . . we see them as the ones that are supposed to be protecting us. That's their role. When that's gone, it's almost like I've got to fend for myself. There's no one out there that's on my side. There's no one out there. . . . I know for some people I've spoken to, my family, cousins, they say they have no one else to rely on. It's . . . if I get into trouble I couldn't depend on you all. I couldn't do it this way. I couldn't call the cops. I couldn't . . . whatever the case may be. It's almost like you have to fend for yourself now. Yeah, they're there. Yeah, I see them driving around but you know what, last time I called them or last time they treated me this way so why bother? You might even go so far as to say that's why people take the law into their own hands. I'll settle this my way. I can't depend on them. They've failed me so many times before.

Edgar's use of "betrayal" is significant because the word denotes a relationship and trust that is broken. He places himself directly in the citizenship realm by identifying himself as a member of the citizenry ("We as citizens . . .") and states an expectation that part of the state's responsibility is protection. Implicit here is a recurring theme that the state is discursively held up as a protector and defender of rights yet causes harm to the citizenry through criminalization processes such as racial profiling. The bulk of his narrative concerns the very practical ramifications for communities of color when they can no longer rely on the state because of anti-citizen experiences. This goes to the alienation and breach of trust generated by racialized social control practices in the racial state.

Carlos argues that distrust of the police due to marginalization of citizenship creates a practical concern of safety for those in need of state services, thus offering insight into one of the mainstays of research on law enforcement and communities of color—the differential in attitudes toward law enforcement across racial and ethnic groups. He states:

> What are your resources after that if you don't feel like you can call? You don't feel like something's going to happen. What if . . . another Hispanic person calls in distress to you and your family? What's going to happen? This is a tough situation we're in.

I asked Carlos how he and his family and friends comprehend and deal with their racialized experiences with the state. He responded that some members of his family tell him to try to "get over" things because that is how they have handled it historically. There is a sense that they must tolerate the mistreatment. I asked him to expand on these concerns:

> I say it's because we're really not Americans. Let's just call it that. We're really not. We're not European. We're not a certain size and eye color. We don't look—even when I went to Panama they said "you're American? That's not what an American looks like—I see them on TV all the time. I know that Americans arrest Mexicans on TV . . . but Americans look differently. They don't look like you." That's the image we're sending out to all of the countries. Well guess what—that's the message we're sending to ourselves. I think because we don't look American—whatever that means—we don't have the same rights. We know that.

Carlos explains that the link between citizenship and whiteness is obvious, given his experience, and those who fall outside of the white bounds of citizenship experience limited rights and protections. His awareness that citizenship is racialized is clear ("we don't look American—whatever that means—we don't have the same rights"). Carlos was one of the more vocal and authoritative respondents when it came to the resistance theme, yet he indicates that the repeated criminalization of communities of color may have a damning, internalizing affect on interactions within the communities.

Jesse invoked the citizenship discourse and the limitations of rights and protections when I asked him to define racial profiling.

> I think about the unequal treatment by the police. I think of abuses of power by the police . . . by abuse of power, it goes more than just overstepping their boundaries. I believe it also deals with not informing the people that they have certain rights, certain liberties. For instance, sometimes cops, they won't let you know that you don't have to do certain things . . . and you'll just do it. Most people are unaware of most of the laws—they just let the police do it. They let the police step all over them because they have no idea of the law.

In the above excerpt, Jesse suggests that the state has an obligation to not take advantage of citizens who may not be fully aware of all of the rights and protections ensured them by the Constitution. Somewhat unique in relation to other criticisms of how the state operates racially, Jesse is pointing out another dimension of state overreach and lack of accountability. Specifically, he refers to the issue of the consent search. Many citizens are not aware that they have the right to refuse a search of their vehicle if asked for a search by law enforcement. Because communities of color are disproportionately stopped by the police, they are also subject to increased searches.[8] The issue of whether contraband (illegal drugs, weapons, etc.) is found in these searches is a null issue for my purposes here although studies suggest there is not a statistically significant difference among groups, particularly with drug offenses that provoke much of the targeted policing in the *war on drugs*.[9] Harcourt provocatively argues that racialized law enforcement leads to more crime overall as whites operate under the premise that they are less likely to receive formal social control from the state (less likely to be stopped and then less likely to be searched when stopped) than are people of color.[10] The consent search issue has prompted discussion among the legal community about the establishment of a *Miranda*-like warning to inform motorists about their right to refuse a search request.[11]

Jesse's account presents another dimension of racialized law enforcement in comparison to an earlier narrative by Darrell. Darrell's narrative, along with others, demonstrated how invoking one's knowledge of the law and due rights of substantive citizenship may bring on increased coercion from the racial state if people of color are viewed as being "out of place" in their assumption of full citizenship. Conversely, Jesse's experience suggests that the state may also act to take advantage of citizens who may not be fully aware of rights and protections that are offered under constitutional guidelines. In either instance, the racial state is maneuvering politically.

Jesse explains how the limitations of citizenship and corresponding resistance to oppression can shape communities of color views of the system.

> Well, if you get angry about it, either A . . . you get . . . if it is destructive anger. . . . I got this chip on my shoulder. It is not pleasant. You think everything is done by the man. All this stick it to the man and all that stuff. None of that really works. You can make it productive, you can take that anger and go do the right [thing]. . . . We live in a bureaucratic system. If you want change, there's bureaucratic ways to do it. You've got to do it and frankly it's hard to do it. We're still going through changes but you know, we are making changes.

Jesse describes himself as resistant to the injustice he experiences as a person of color and how his anger toward white supremacy can be both stifling and enabling, depending on how one uses the energy. His account points to a sense of commitment to the collective community, a recognition that the personal is political, as well as to more generalized notions of citizenship. Within this context of a collective community and a "bureaucratic system," Jesse makes a call to others to make changes in the citizenship realm, stating that it "has to be done" and will be "difficult." This last passage falls under the resistance mode that calls for taking action—tangible and political—in the lives of others as well as in one's own life.

Another respondent who was particularly resistant to racialization and criminalization processes and whose community activism centered along relations with the police in her community was Angela, a black female in her fifties (she did not offer her educational background). In the next passage, Angela is following up on a story she relayed about mistreatment by the police and how she went up the chain of command for accountability ("everyone has a boss"), thus resisting in a direct confrontation with institutional power, in addition to making tangible, political changes in others' lives:

> I myself, the way I was raising my children, I voiced that opinion to them a lot. If something comes up with a police officer, and they feel like they can't talk to that police officer, they have a right to ask for their superior. Because everybody has a boss. That's what I teach them.

Darrell, when asked about resistance to racialized policing, focused on how knowing one's rights are key. Darrell understands that for the white citizenry, when the state does overextend its boundaries on rights and protections, (white) mechanisms generally exist to hold the state accountable. In the lengthy segment that follows, he talks about options he felt he had in dealing with a police officer with a history of harassing him and his friends when he was younger. Darrell's comments highlight the many facets of accountability. Once an incident of police abuse of authority or force occurs, the added grievance of not having the injustice addressed appropriately is part of the experience for many people of color. In fact, the lack of accountability following an injustice is in some ways more damaging than the original violation of citizenship rights and protections. That is, the checks and balances that constitute a fair criminal justice system are seen as failing for communities of color.[12] In addition, Darrell suggests that the repercussions in those cases when justice does prevail complicate the rewards of justice that might otherwise arise.

> We converse about it. Debate what is best . . . our recourse. As teenagers, of course, how much influence could we have? We knew our parents had more. We spoke with our parents. You're looking at children who already had strikes against them being young, being black, being in not the most impoverished neighborhoods but one of poverty, definitely. You're looking at children who are like, we'll tell our parents. They're going to go complain, they're going to have the fallout for the complaints that they've made. You're already able and mature enough to understand that sometimes that's how things work. My mother goes and says something and they are harassing her. My father goes and says something, they're gonna harass him. Like I said, those ills, those social ills are already in place to

> where they have stolen our mental freedom to where we already knew. If we complain, it's going to get worse! If you say something, it's going to get worse than it was before. It came to the point, for lack of a better word, we developed tolerance for it. Put up with it. We never liked it. Never enjoyed it, not one bit, but we dealt with it. That's just, that's life for us. In our world, anyway.
>
> If they are held accountable, what about the repercussions afterwards? I still live here. My family still lives here. It's terrible. Like I said, that goes back to freedom. For your mind. It's very hard to walk around your town for God knows how many years, knowing that if you've had something go down with law enforcement officials, and its gone too far and it does pan out in your favor, they're held accountable. . . . I still have a small victory from the war. I've won a small battle but on the front lines, they're still kicking butt. I'm taking too many casualties. That's how it is. That's still winning. Resources for them are more available. . . . That's how I feel. It's a very oppressive feeling, you know? As if, well hell, they're not going to get anything anyway. Nothing's going to happen to them. I can complain. I can moan. They're not going to do anything but take the public relations route and wiggle their way out.

An examination of Darrell's use of metaphor offers insight into how the struggle over rights, protections, and accountability in police–minority relations manifests. Darrell engages the discourse of warfare to illustrate the combative nature of the relationship. Even though the officer who made the initial arrest, and with whom Darrell had a history of harassment, was let go from the police force a short while after Darrell's arrest, Darrell describes this development as "a small *victory* from *the war*." He tells of how he feels as if he were "on the front lines" and "taking . . . casualties." Even though he linked this officer's departure to his unsubstantiated arrest, Darrell still views the state as "winning" in the long run and remarks on the "oppressive feeling" he has when reflecting upon the issue. Outside of the nonsubstantive citizenship realm where Darrell's experiences lie, (white) citizens are less likely to experience the state as a formidable opponent with which they associate being against on the "front lines." Indeed, in the race-neutral world of citizenship, when warfare discourse is engaged it is generally in the context of state efforts at the protection of the citizenry!

Darrell's view that one of the hallmarks of citizenship—accountability—is out of reach for many people of color prompts a passionate response when asked about the responsibility of the state in addressing injustices. As a citizen, he shines the spotlight of accountability on himself and his community as well because of the reciprocal responsibilities he understands theoretically should exist in the citizen–state dyad. He also illustrates how people of color, particularly young men of color, must constantly negotiate the racial terrain of the state to get themselves and loved ones out of potentially threatening situations with law enforcement.

> Nothing's going to change. Nothing's gonna be done no matter how much we rally, you know. No matter how much we speak up and protest. There aren't going to be any repercussions. So I believe, just to give a flip on that, as individuals, we need to be more accountable for ourselves and our actions. Just try our best to stay out of harm's way when we're in those situations. I'm not saying that we can avoid the other variables when we're stopped and we're seething. I've been there! I've been there to the point where I've been seething so bad that they called backup, so I know. When you're in those situations just try to stop that effect because you already know the deck of cards are stacked against you. Be accountable for your actions because it's not that they aren't going to be caught in the act of going too far on their end or whatever but the chances seem so much less on their end, you know, as far as them being held accountable for their actions and the individual being held for theirs. They're the law. Accountability? Accountability for who? For who? Not them especially.

Darrell continues with the line of thought regarding the layers of protections assumed in the roles of the family institution and the state. *Parens patriae*, the concept that the state is bound to look out for the well-being of its citizens (particularly the young), is invoked though obviously overridden by the noncitizen role that Darrell views himself in given his experiences with the state.

> Your parents are your first line of defense when you're born. Those individuals are your first line of defense as far as protecting you and sheltering from harm and teaching you rights and wrongs of society. Then you have laws in place by man of course to help keep peace in society. It's that structure. When you get out of the house when you get older and you finally go out onto the world on your own, you're out of your parents' and guardians' protection. Here you are dealing with the world on your own as an individual, an independent individual. You run into so many things that you couldn't have been prepared for by your parents and guardians. It's just—it's nerve-racking. It's truly psychological warfare. They, whoever they are, who put these laws in place, who put these regulations to critique people's appetites for more freedom or for "comfortability" in their freedom already—they're winning.

Carlos explains how the use of force entrusted in the state becomes a concern under racialization and criminalization processes like racial profiling. He makes a connection between everyday race-based behaviors, i.e., "it is across the board . . ." and race-based behavior on behalf of agents of the state authorized to use force.

> It is wrong. It is very much discriminating to profile according to race. And it is across the board. . . . The problem is with police, it goes from being wrong to potentially being deadly. They are an authority. They have weapons. They have the right to use force and they could justify all of their actions. I think

> that when police and men in those situations in authority use that, it could be very dangerous. Especially to minorities.

As noted, another aspect of the citizenship realm that the respondents engage is the collective. There is a sense of concern for other people of color who are subjected to racial profiling, thus, in a pure sense of citizenship, these respondents are able to look beyond their own personal experience when examining racial profiling. The strategy of resistance about the personal being political is evident. In the passage below, Carlos comments on status markers that may facilitate racial injustice.

> We're not a great pick of the community. We look differently, you know? We're educated. You look at the community and the guys maybe look differently. They have tattoos that are very visible. They dress differently. They have stories about getting pulled over and getting pulled out of the car. Every time. What do they do? It's upsetting because I don't want to be treated like that. I certainly don't want my son treated that way. I will do everything I have to and if that means donating more money to police departments to get a sticker. . . . That's what I gotta do as ridiculous as that sounds. I don't really wanna. I don't want to take the easy way out.
>
> The power, the authority and their guns . . . then they have their own chips on their shoulder. They're upset with things they see. They get to go out [and] take it out on us. They know that. They're not gonna pull that white kid out and mess with him. They're not because he has a job, he has connections, and he might know someone who he might tell. Let's say another 15-year-old is pulled over. Who is he gonna tell? He's already been in trouble. The judge knows his name. They know who they can—every now and then they mess it up. They cross the line. That's when you hear about it on the news. I'm saying I think this happens way more than we even think. They are select targets. . . . It's just upsetting. We're striving to get better and get educated.

His concern is not limited to himself or even his young son but goes to the broader community of color who are subject to criminalization and racialization processes by the state. He expresses clear concern about accountability. He argues that there is a differential enforcement of the law that goes against the citizenship ideals of equal justice and that whiteness provides some protection against injustices by the state. Carlos recognizes that his adherence to the citizenship ideal, for instance his reference to his college education, is not a protective mechanism against anti-citizenship practices, and other markers of status provide even less protection.

Hector, a Latino in his forties with a high school education, engages the justice and liberty rights frame as he espouses an ultra-patriotic discourse verging on hyperbole to frame his discontent with the citizen–state relationship:

> I know I'm an American because I was born here. I went to school here. I was educated here. I'm as American as anybody else. Red, white, and blue—that's all I bleed. For them to come up and question me as far as that. . . . I'm not a citizen of the United States. I'm disenfranchised!

Later, he again invokes the term "disenfranchised," defined as a loss of rights and protections, and says that his experiences make him feel like he is "not a part of this country." This is clearly in the DuBoisian sense of the "American" identity clashing with identity as a person of color in the eyes of the racial state. As with other respondents, throughout the interview he is credentialing and self-defining the situation by rejecting the criminal identity imposed on him by the state.

> When people of a different race, particularly white police officers in this town, look at me and see my tattoos, they automatically assume that I've been to prison, I'm involved in a gang. They don't look at me as the human being that I am. I go to church every Sunday. . . . I'm a member in good standing. I own a business and it is in good standing. Unless they . . . they don't realize . . . they automatically assume because I'm Hispanic and I have a tattoo that I'm either dealing drugs or hanging out with a gang or just got out of the pen.

Jerome, a black male in his forties with a graduate degree and a former police officer, also tells of how living up to citizenship ideals does not necessarily mean the state will fulfill its part of the social contract. While this particular incident is not specifically about a traffic stop (he says elsewhere in the interview that he has had *dozens* of stops over his lifetime), it is about criminalization processes in the black community. He tells of an encounter outside of his home in which a police officer responding to a possible prowler call mistakenly targeted Jerome, going so far as to unsnap his gun holster (an official use of force action in many jurisdictions) as Jerome was taking out diaper-filled trash bags from his newborn daughter.

> My hands was holding two trash bags full of doo-doo. Manure. Trash. I dropped it. How could I be having anything in my hand? You read about black people getting shot—they didn't have anything in their hand! A lot of white officers are scared of black people. They need to have some kind of sensitivity training to deal with us. We're not animals. If we live on the south side, we have to get there through work, education, class, social economic . . . whatever you want to call it. By me talking about it, it makes me really mad because you read about justice for all. It's not justice for all. That's what really saddens me about America sometimes. No I don't want to move to another country. I love America. I was born here. But I'm saying we have a lot of flaws and until we straighten out those flaws, it's going to continue to be like that.

Jerome's initial comments go to the sense of danger people of color, particularly men of color, need be concerned with in the encounters with the racial state. Employing the self-definition and self-valuation mode of resistance, Jerome counters the criminalization process by accessing the situation within the context of his experience as a law enforcement officer. He also engages in credentialing with his reference to working hard and playing by society's rules to get where he is today (the south side of town is a predominantly white, upper socioeconomic status area of the city). As dangerous as his encounter with the officer was, his assessment of it quickly goes beyond the incident itself. The "justice for all" reference points to a clear engagement of citizenship discourse and the DuBoisian awareness of limited citizenship for people of color.

Jerome's comments reveal another dimension of the citizenship realm for people of color. Those who speak out against racialized social control practices of the state even though they "love America" are subject to the "America—love it or leave it" mentality and accompanying efforts to alienate them. These attacks on critics who bring injustices to light are rarely viewed as attempts to *defend* the Constitution and its promise of equal protection under the law. Yet the upholding of the promise of equal treatment under the law is indeed what these efforts aim to accomplish. Jerome expresses a realistic sadness at the contradictions encompassed in the constitutional realm for communities of color.

Francis, a black woman in her fifties with some college education, adds yet another dimension of racialized social control practices experienced collectively by communities of color. Like several of the respondents (particularly female respondents) who have sons, her concerns about the experiences young men of color have with law enforcement in the contemporary era take center stage. This reflects how part of citizenship is recognizing the broader social context one belongs to, thus reflective of Collins's resistance awareness that the personal is political. For people of color, personal experiences like a racialized traffic stop can only fully be understood within the broader realm of racial minority status in a white-dominated society. In the excerpt below, Francis is responding to a general inquiry about instances where racial and ethnic status figured into an encounter with law enforcement.

> I've seen incidents where policemens have searched, looking for one person, and have really searched the whole group of black boys when they claim they are looking for one . . . that they are not looking for this one certain person yet still they are . . . having them all against fences and things which kind of upset the blacks because we figure they wouldn't be doing nobody else's child like that. I've had incidents where they've all, the children, have told us about how police treats them, talks to them, kind of demanding and

> making them say things they didn't want to say . . . which is also against us because mostly we feel like . . . they're picking on our black kids.

Part of the reciprocal nature of the relationship between the state and the citizen lies in the autonomy of the individual, yet citizenship also entails a simultaneous concern for the collective within which the individual is situated. Francis's remarks that the "whole group" of young boys are subjected to state intervention via a physical search demonstrates the criminalization of black male youth as a collective and how they are not extended full individual protections from the state. Francis directly frames the citizenship issue in the context of unequal treatment by the state—"we figure they wouldn't be doing nobody else's child like that." She also speaks to coercive techniques employed by the state when dealing with young people in her community. Francis views this behavior as unequal treatment under the law and as a direct reflection of the state's broader treatment of communities of color. Clearly Francis possesses the double consciousness and insight DuBois describes as characteristic of communities of color.

In the following, Francis prefaces her observations on the experiential nature of racial inequality by engaging the citizenship discourse.

> I know you got to respect the law but I don't think it takes all of that to get your point over or to make them [the citizenry] respect you. . . . Matter of fact, they got me to where I don't want to support them in nothing they do . . . because when you look at it, they are so rude, so rude. Other folks talk about how they do. . . . When we go along with what we hear, what we see, what we are experiencing with our own kids . . . we don't, we just don't like it. . . . It's just something I wouldn't want nobody to go through and I can't really see how anybody would have a heart to do this (emphatic) . . . when all kids—whether they are black, white, yellow, green—whatever color they are, male or female. . . . I just can't see nobody being treated like this.

The citizenship discourse begins with Francis's acknowledgment that folks have to "respect the law" then quickly critiques the state's actions as alienating. The experiential nature of racism is evident in Francis's comments about "what we hear, what we see, and what we [experience]" with racialized encounters with the state. The account from Francis also reflects a general pattern in the data that the female respondents were less able to discuss personal experiences with a racialized traffic stop than they were able to discuss more general racialization and criminalization processes in their communities. Clearly, this is a reflection of the racialized and gendered nature of racial profiling.

A primary aspect of the citizenship discourse concerns the "contractual" obligations present in the citizen–state relationship. Individuals who show what Hirschi classically refers to as commitment and conformity to society and are ideally given for exchange, certain grants of citizenship. Victor, a Latino in his twenties with some college education, discusses how stereotyping processes associated with racialization limit his access to citizenship.

> If you're black, a lot of people will think that you're just a thug, that you listen to rap music. They're going to pigeonhole you into a particular box. If you're Hispanic, you love Tejano music or any of that sort. There are certain ways that people look at you. That you are lazy. That you are a procrastinator. You don't want to work. That you just want to come over here and abuse the system. That's not it at all. I was born there. I was a migrant worker. I joined the military. I became a United States citizen. I graduated high school. I'm going to college. I'm not living off the system. I'm a prime example of what we don't want to be. We want to be looked at as individuals. Everybody does, no matter what color or race you are. But you're still in a society that is not willing to let go.

In this passage the linkage between immigrant status and citizenship is evident. For Latinos, there is an added dimension to fulfilling the ideals of citizenship. Many Latinos not only experience limited citizenship treatment from the state in the more abstract sense of not receiving the grant of substantive citizenship, but are also subject to very practical nativity concerns about foreign-born status. Victor lists many of the stereotypes identified with Latinos then counters those representations in credentialing and self-defining his personal experiences that indeed are reflective of all of the ideals of citizenship.

At another point, Victor discusses how these criminalization processes interfere with his everyday life. He relays a story about returning from a movie with his light-skinned Latina girlfriend and his younger, dark-skinned brothers in the car. After being stopped by the police and having his future wife asked to get out of the car, Victor gets no response from two officers when he, as a citizen, asks for the reason for the stop.

> When my wife came back into the vehicle, I asked her what was the problem. She explained to me that the other police officer had stated to her that there was a call made by a girl, a white girl, that there was four Hispanic males threatening her that they were going to kidnap her and rape her. I mean that's—it just made me so angry. I was in a neighborhood where not very many white people live, for one. Just to deal with that first hand was kind of weird at first. I didn't feel too angry at the very beginning. I felt maybe they just made a mistake, an honest mistake, because she looks a certain way. Regardless, towards the end, it was a feeling of anger and like it wasn't right for them to do that. There was no probable cause.

During this part of the interview, Victor was noticeably upset. Although he doesn't question the somewhat outlandish story given to his girlfriend about the reason for the stop, his account makes clear that racial and ethnic concerns shape his everyday encounters as he comments on the skin tone of the actors involved in his story, describes the racial surroundings of the encounter, and questions the motivations of officers by initially giving them the benefit of the doubt. He initially resists the double-consciousness realm but, upon reflection of the incident, he invokes the citizenship realm by his claim that it "wasn't right" for the officers to make contact because of the lack of probable cause. Invoking this Fourth Amendment canon is a direct call to citizenship and the liberty and justice rights frame.

Evident in Victor's narrative is a sense that although many people of color may have expectations of limited citizenship by the state because of experiential racism, they are not necessarily prejudging encounters with law enforcement ("I felt maybe they just made a mistake . . ."). Another example comes from Manuel, a Latino in his forties with some college, who was recently released from prison after being incarcerated for a number of years. Throughout the interview, Manuel returns to the idea that concerns he has about law enforcement and racial profiling were unfounded. Because he had a criminal record and thus was guilty of criminal behavior in the past, Manuel thought he may be paranoid about the criminal justice system and that the police are not really targeting him because of his ethnicity. Subtle references to living up to the ideals of good citizenship—showing commitment to society among them—however, indicate that Manuel views his postprison life as one in which he demonstrates the traits of a good citizen yet still experiences marginalizing treatment from the state. In the excerpt below, Manuel has just given an account of an encounter with law enforcement in which he believed the officer indicated Manuel did not "belong" in the area. I asked him about the out-of-place doctrine that shapes his everyday experiences.

> I think it gives me an attitude of wanting to rebel. Cause I'm like . . . I'm trying to do right, right? Like I told you where I came from and what I've done. But even though I'm trying to do the best that I can, there's always something that's gonna try to pull me back. I catch myself wondering—what are you talking about? What am I doing? In other words, it gets me mad 'cause . . . here I am just trying to be cool, go about whatever I'm doing, whatever I'm doing but I stick out like a sore thumb. So I've got to catch myself sometimes and I got to say, hey, whoa.

Manuel recognizes that his alienation from the state is not simply a matter of his criminal past. He self-defines the situation and knows that his exemplary postprison behavior places him in an upstanding position in the citizenry (he is a "model" reformed convict), yet his status as a Latino forces him into the nonsubstantive citizenship realm.

Pam, a black female in her thirties with a college degree, focused most of her comments on an issue that had filled up much of her time over the previous several months—the incarceration of her brother. Convinced that her brother was convicted unjustly because of issues of race and socioeconomic status, Pam and her family enjoys the support of the Innocence Project on this case. While this respondent's narrative is not directly one about the effects of a criminalizing traffic stop, Pam does offer insight into the more general processes of racialization and criminalization in the criminal justice system that undermines the citizen–state relationship. In the following narrative, she responds to a question about her view of law enforcement and the criminal justice system at large prior to the situation with her brother.

> You know I've never been in a situation to even think about it but if I can reflect back I probably think I just gave them the benefit of the doubt. Whatever happened—those people are guilty, they found them guilty. That was my attitude on it pretty much until I actually had first-hand experience with it [racism in the criminal justice system]. I would normally say it is a crutch people were using just because it didn't turn out in their favor. Then I experienced it first hand.

Pam provides another example of how communities of color do not have a monolithic view of the criminal justice system and indeed have dynamic views of the system. This is in contrast to some of the discourse surrounding communities of color and crime that characterize minorities as opposed to *law and order*. The discursive framing of communities of color as contesting law and law enforcement helps facilitate their alienation from the system. Pam's remarks also suggest that she had adopted some of the ideology surrounding racism—that people of color may play "the race card" when things don't go "in their favor." Yet, her experiences in the legal realm disprove her earlier notions of the fairness of the system.

Another respondent also focused her remarks on the incarceration of a family member. Barbara, a multiracial woman in her fifties with some college education, expressed great concern about the quality of legal representation her son received on the heels of very minimal and circumstantial evidence that brought him to trial. Barbara described the everydayness of racism in the post-Civil Rights era as "sneaky" and "so good at hiding," particularly in the legal realm: "It's nothing that you can pinpoint. It's nothing that you can say definitely. It's a feeling, it's a hearing. . . . If you could prove this, then there wouldn't be a problem. But you can't prove it."

I asked Barbara if prior to the situation with her son and the criminal justice system, she believed in the system and its accompanying citizenship discourse of equal justice.

> Oh yeah. I was very trusting. Very, very trusting in the system—and verbal about it. I was here to say that we have the best system in the world because of our Constitution. Because it says that you are innocent until proven guilty and that everyone has the right to a fair trial. I believed all of these things. They taught you all of this in civics class and this is the way the law is. Being naïve to the law, I accepted it. I don't accept it now.
>
> I was a good American citizen. . . . I look at so many things now so differently. I look at everything differently. It's not the same world. I'm not the same person. Sometimes I think I want to be that Barbara again but . . . no, I don't because my eyes were closed because I believed. I believed we have a good system and we don't.

In this narrative, Barbara supports the earlier view of Pam that communities of color do embrace the liberty and justice rights frame characterized by the ideology of democracy, citizenship, and freedom. Again, DuBois's concern with double-consciousness is evident: People of color generally hold firm to the ideals of citizenship, understand that it is due to them, yet simultaneously recognize that in practice, full citizenship is often denied. Barbara explains that she viewed the criminal justice system as one about fairness and embodied in the Constitution. She clearly links her prior view of the system to early socialization processes. Her self-identity as a "good American citizen," however, is shaken when she experiences the break from citizenship emergent in racialization and criminalization processes inherent to the American criminal justice system. The lenses of citizenship changed for Barbara, both at the micro ("I'm not the same person") and macro ("It's not the same world"). Although this example is not directly related to racial profiling concerns as they manifest in the traffic stop, it encompasses the fundamental issues—racialization and criminalization—of racial profiling. Barbara also demonstrates resistance to the racism she and her family encountered by refusing to continue to accept the justice and liberty frame that had shaped her view of the system.

CONCLUSION

This chapter demonstrates that the personal experience of people of color in racialized encounters with law enforcement go well beyond the local, micro-level association focused on in the current racial profiling literature. My respondents clearly reflect on these encounters as racializing and criminalizing experiences with the state that are experienced as watershed moments in their lives. The overarching theme that emerges from their narratives is one of a break from citizenship and the liberty and justice rights frame that encompasses it. In other examinations of how race operates in the criminal justice system, this process is referred to as an "attenuation" of citizenship.[13] Western, in his examination of the role and effects of status differentials in regards to incarceration, views the effects of race and socioeconomic status as an "evolutionary" aspect of African American citizenship because of the *retrenchment* of citizenship.[14] Yet, as shown by the active and frequent engagement of the "liberty and justice" rights frame by many of my respondents, people of color continue to make claim to the citizenship realm and resist the denial of full citizenship by the racial state. Writing in the late 1800s, DuBois described this same struggle to reconcile the "warring ideals" of minority identity and citizen identity imposed by the racial state with the self-identified sense of being a full citizen.[15]

The narratives in the current chapter build on the idea of resisting the anti-citizenship identity imposed by the state. Through an analysis that primarily engages Collins's resistance strategies, I show how my respondents incorporate both direct and indirect modes of opposition to racial profiling processes inherent in the racial state. A hallmark of the resistance is critical consciousness and insight into the ways of a racial state that whites do not possess. While the current racial profiling literature approaches the notion of citizenship superficially via the procedural justice framework (concerned with the fairness of treatment during traffic stops), mainstream criminology has yet to examine any aspects of resistance to racial profiling, clearly a dominant narrative from respondents in my analysis.

The next chapter will pick up the theme of vicarious experience as it is the other main factor mainstream criminology forwards as a determinant in what makes individuals perceive they have been racially profiled. I examine qualitatively the meaning and lived experiences behind the vicarious experience variable by an initial theoretical engagement of panopticonism and double-consciousness, followed by incorporation of the concepts of collective memory and the lesson.

NOTES

1. See Appendix A for details on methods and Appendix B for the interview schedule.
2. Russell, Katheryn K. 1998. *The Color of Crime: Racial Hoaxes, White Fear, Black Protectionism, Police Harassment, and Other Macroaggressions*. New York: New York University Press.
3. Collins, Patricia Hill. 2000. *Black Feminist Thought: Knowledge, Consciousness, and the Politics of Empowerment*. New York: Routledge.
4. Russell, *The Color of Crime*.

5. Withrow, Brian L. 2006. *Racial Profiling: From Rhetoric to Reason*. Upper Saddle River, NJ: Pearson-Prentice Hall.

6. Feagin, Joe R. 2006. *Systemic Racism: A Theory of Oppression*. New York: Routledge.

7. Mills, Charles W. 1997. *The Racial Contract*. Ithaca, NY: Cornell University Press.

8. Withrow, *Racial Profiling*.

9. Withrow, *Racial Profiling*; Harcourt, Bernard E. 2007. *Against Prediction: Profiling, Policing, and Punishing in an Actuarial Age*. Chicago: University of Chicago Press.

10. Harcourt, *Against Prediction*.

11. Withrow, *Racial Profiling*.

12. Russell, *The Color of Crime*.

13. Pettit, Becky, and Bruce Western. 2004. "Mass Imprisonment and the Life Course: Race and Class Inequality in U.S. Incarceration." *American Sociological Review* 69: 151–69.

14. Western, Bruce. 2006. *Punishment and Inequality in America*. New York: Russell Sage Foundation.

15. DuBois, W. E. B. 1986. *Writings: The Suppression of the Slave Trade; The Souls of Black Folks; Dusk of Dawn; Essays and Articles*. New York: Literary Classics of the United States-Library of America, p. 364.

7

Vicarious Experience, Panopticonism, and Oral History

Racial matters operate in the real lives of black and white people, not in sentimental caverns of the mind.

Derrick Bell[1]

Recent work on racial profiling suggests that vicarious experiences are influential in shaping attitudes toward the police and in shaping individuals' understanding of racial profiling experiences (i.e., have I been racially profiled?). Vicarious experiences include information about profiling from family and friends and may be defined as the imagined participation in others' experiences. Leading studies described vicarious experience as internalizing another person's experience that "may then be communicated to yet other friends, family members, acquaintances, and neighbors—amplifying the effect of the initial experience and perhaps influencing beliefs about the police within a whole network of people. . . ."[2]

Implicit in some of the discourse surrounding vicarious experience is that an individual who has not experienced racial profiling personally may adopt certain perspectives on citizen–state relations even if they themselves have not had negative experiences. In other discourses on racial and ethnic status more generally, a running theme is that if communities of color, particularly blacks, stopped discussing slavery and other overt examples of racial oppression (often denoted as relics of the past), then younger generations could "get over" the idea that racial oppression is widespread in contemporary America.[3] In other racialized contexts, such as described in Moore's critical examination of racial dynamics in elite law schools, discourse from law students of color about how the law operates racially is discounted by white students.[4] The currently ill-developed notion of vicarious experience in the literature engages, if subtlety, the traditional complaint from whites that people of color *play the race card* (never mind that the largest playing of race cards is that of whiteness) at times when events or circumstances are not actually racialized. To extend this notion, vicarious experience may be contextualized as another example of playing the race card. Specifically, I argue, because vicarious experience by definition does not actually involve genuine experience with a phenomenon, the inherent importance of the phenomenon may be diminished. Critical examination of the focus on vicarious experiences by mainstream researchers suggests a subtle tendency in this direction: Communities of color views of the police arise in part because the community collectively keeps stories of police abuse of authority alive through oral histories and neighborhood gripe sessions that undermine what may be an otherwise acceptable relationship with the state. Examination of the process of informational exchange that does not engage a race theory lens may view this collective dialogue as limiting efforts to move beyond America's racial history. The focus by mainstream criminology on the vicarious experience component of racial profiling is an example of the white logic that Zuberi and Bonilla-Silva argue shapes much of social science.[5] As such, a critical race framework that addresses racial profiling as racial oppression is necessary to rearrange the logic of the scholarship addressing the racial profiling experience. As demonstrated in the analysis to follow, vicariousness is a complex part of the racial profiling experience and goes beyond the orientation of mainstream research and its tendency to position social actors as relatively passive individuals who lack agency.

COLLECTIVE MEMORY AND "THE LESSON"

I suggest it is necessary to analyze racial profiling and the vicarious experience factor through what is known as "the lesson."[6] Part of the collective memory that Feagin[7] and others discuss as a connected communal awareness of past racial injustices that forge and assist in explaining contemporary racial realities, the lesson refers to guidance and advice offered among communities of color, generally from older members of the community to younger generations. The guidance often comes in the form of admonitions about contact with law enforcement during traffic stops, and more generally about contact with the state. Keeping hands in plain view on the steering wheel, making no sudden movements, and being extraordinarily polite to officers in order to get oneself out of a potentially dangerous situation are critical points comprising the lesson. While white parents and community members also instill a sense of obedience to authority and law enforcement generally, the efforts of communities of color in engaging the lesson generation after generation suggests that the consequences of not following the sage advice are more dire than for white communities. Contemporary examples abound of police use of force with people of color that include rationalization by the police that they feared for their safety when later the victim was found to be unarmed (e.g., Amadou Diallo). Due to associations with criminality and violence that people of color, especially young males, encounter in society, law enforcement is more willing to engage in force with racial minorities than with whites.[8]

Vicarious experiences are not simply about hearing from friends and family that an injustice has occurred. From a critical perspective, vicarious experience is more about efforts within communities of color to support one another when dealing with systems of oppression, like the criminal justice system. It is a way of communicating historical and contemporary realities that are determinant in relations with the state. Ultimately, the lesson is very purpose-driven communication dealing directly with matters of life and death.

Contextualizing the three issues of vicarious experience, panopticonism, and oral history into the racial profiling realm is important for a number of reasons. Panopticonism sets the historical precedent and contemporary reality for personal and vicarious experiences that get communicated across generations via the lesson. Vicarious experiences may operate on some level to perpetuate historical animosities in police–minority relations but it is unlikely that these histories remain intrinsically important collectively if *contemporary* experiences don't back them up. Thus, the lesson persists as a way communities of color guide future generations in the midst of the panopticon experience in a racial state.

The following analysis of data looks at all three of these issues together. Specifically, when a respondent comments on the regularity of racialization and criminalization processes, I consider this as part of the panopticon effect—this awareness of constantly being evaluated for criminality. It may also involve the general awareness of injustice in black and Latino communities that is discussed, examined, and resisted among members of the community. In addition, the dominant narrative addressed in the previous chapter—citizenship—is also engaged in the current chapter because of its salience to racial profiling experiences.

SILENT NO MORE: VICARIOUS EXPERIENCE, PANOPTICONISM, DOUBLE CONSCIOUSNESS, AND "THE LESSON"

I begin with Darrell, a black male in his twenties with some college education, as he introduces all three ideas in the following lengthy excerpt. As with all respondents, my opening question was how they defined racial profiling and what the concept meant to them. Darrell's initial response included the notion of freedom. I asked him to expand on that idea in the context of racial profiling.

> Just to be free in general is to be unbound. To be unshackled. It doesn't matter whether that means metaphorically speaking, mentally, or physically. Just to be free means not to be bound by anyone or anything, basically. When you put that stress on individuals with certain types of laws or hidden rules that hinders their freedom. It makes their freedom even harder to be enjoyed. Racial profiling definitely does it. With me anyway, being a young man of true African American descent—I'm only three generations out of Africa. So being a young man that knows that . . . I get to listen to my grandfather on my mother's side and my grandfather on my father's side is still alive. These are men who have been through the storm, so to speak, and know what has happened, what is happening, and they can pretty much almost in a psychic kind of sense, tell you what will happen.
>
> My grandfathers always tell me one, that there's no need for you to, you know, let it bother you to an extent. More so than it should. They want me to know that it is the world we live in. No, excuse me—it's the people in the world we live in. They let me know that it's not my fault and to understand that until these ills are corrected, it's just something that's gonna be happening in our world. They've been racially profiled many times. My mother's father is 82 years old. My father's father is in his late 60s. They still are very wise and inform me a lot. They've been through a lot. A lot of similarities between their cases. They've seen so many things that it would take another lifetime of interviews to explain what I've been able to learn from them and draw out of it.
>
> They said to be careful. Don't give them any reason—more than what they already have or feel that they have to follow you—to do anything stupid towards you. Just cooperate. Don't be upset. You have every right to be upset if you haven't done anything and they're stopping you just because. So I believe that with that being said, I've been able to take that and thankfully I haven't had a plethora of problems but I've had my share. The sad thing about it is a lot of people look at it and they don't realize how much racial profiling or whatever the term may be is more psychological warfare than anything.

Darrell's use of metaphor is particularly meaningful. The imagery produced through his selection of "unbound" and "unshackled" clearly posit the racial profiling experience within the context of slavery. Foucault's idea of corporal punishment and social control via the public execution is easily extended to the realm of the corporal nature of slavery.[9] Foucault views the panopticon experience as one released from the body but one that effectively binds the mind. From Foucault, the move in governance from one concerned with the body to one concerned with the mind, consciousness, and the soul are evident in Darrell's remarks. Foucault suggests that while both the mind and the body were bound in early times, the effect of the panopticon ushered in a "shift in the point of application of this power: It is no longer the body, with the ritual play of excessive pains, spectacular brandings in the ritual of the public execution; it is the mind or rather a play of representations and signs circulating discreetly but necessarily and evidently in the minds of all. It is no longer the body, but the soul. . . ."[10] Darrell associates the constant surveillance of racial profiling with governance of the body during the slavery era. Later he makes reference to "mental freedom," a concept very much in the realm of what Foucault argued was lacking as a consequence of panoptic social control.

His grandparents' advice is an excellent example of how the lesson operates for communities of color. First, the experiences of the elders are valued as accounts of how those who go through "the storm" develop a knowledge base of racial oppression that is viewed as a source of strength. Collins's[11] notion that personal troubles are politically constituted is evident in Darrell's grandfathers' wisdom that the injustice of criminalization processes is a product of "the world we live in." The expression is also suggestive of the panopticon and the consistency of its effects. There is an emphasis on behaving in a manner that will not result in dangerous confrontation. The historical reality of police–minority relations necessitates this informational exchange as a matter of survival. Yet, as evidence of resistance and awareness of the oppression, the elders engage the liberty and justice rights discourse ("you have every right to be upset if you haven't done anything") to support Darrell in his position as a citizen. Finally, Darrell's use of warfare discourse is informative. It illustrates Foucault's concern that constant surveillance and the panopticon effect impact the psyche. In this instance, it is particularly striking because outside of the anti-citizen realm in which he and many other people of color exist in practice, warfare discourse is invoked when the state is engaged in *protecting* the citizen, not in causing harm to the citizen.

The narrative clearly demonstrates how the guidance and advice coming from the elders is not relayed as a purposeful effort to negatively shape young Darrell's view of the state. Rather, the guidance is presented as sage advice about how best to operate in a racial state. These admonitions help prepare young people for the racism they will likely face in that racial state.

The consistency of the panopticon effect is evident in another excerpt from Darrell. I asked him to expand on his idea that racial profiling was a form of "psychological warfare."

> Oh because when you're expecting to be stopped just because of your ethnicity, of your age demographic or just the way you look. Mentally you have that in the back of your mind—it can happen at any time. So you sit up and think,

> well man! . . . So it's a psychological thing because here you are a human being and that's taking away a large piece of your mental freedom because you know you're going to get stopped. You don't know when. You don't know under what circumstances. Even when it does go down, you don't know how far they're going to go with the stop. . . . It cheats an individual out of some of their mental freedom because you have to worry about that.
>
> There's an uncomfortable state of mind that you attain when you go through something like that. So if you've experienced it once and you get stopped later on down the road again and you've done nothing, not necessarily the same circumstances but the same atmosphere of behavior. Here we go again. I'm clean. I haven't done anything. I'm getting stopped. . . . So there's a very uncomfortable state of mind that you experience when you go through something like that. So you don't forget that, you know? You can't just block that out of your mind. I think you have to be delusional to say "Well it will be different next time." And actually believe that fully . . . you can think that . . . but you're not going to fully believe it. I don't believe you can. I haven't. I never will again.

Darrell makes several references to the mental burden of constant surveillance. DuBois's double-consciousness concept is an appropriate frame in respondent references to the duality they face as both Americans and people of color. In this instance, Darrell signals his citizenship in its guarantee of "mental freedom," yet through racialization and criminalization processes inherent to racial profiling recognizes a distinct lack of "freedom" because of his racial status. By engaging citizenship ideals (the ability to have mental freedom) and recognizing the limitations placed on him, Darrell is aware of the *two-ness* DuBois argues is both a burdensome, negative condition of people of color and, in the same instance, an insight that allows people of color to see the world *as it really is,* a world that whites do not comprehend nor possess. There is a sense that the struggle between citizenship and minority status invoked by panopticonism in a racial state, when acknowledged, may either be "debilitating" or "emancipating."[12]

Darrell's remarks offer a good example of the Foucaultian premise of the panopticon effect: "to induce . . . a state of conscious and permanent visibility that assures the automatic functioning of power . . . the surveillance is permanent in its effects, even if it is discontinuous in its action." Darrell describes how the panopticon experience involves a dispersion of discreet "representations and signs" that cause social actors under the panopticon effect to be hyperaware of state-centered surveillance. Again, Darrell refers to the psychological and the "worry" that accompanies ubiquitous surveillance. He is even compelled to qualify his remarks with the comment that he is a "human being." The panopticon effect is demonstrated in the expectation of being stopped "in the back of your mind—it can happen at any time." Whites are not encumbered with a similar expectation of unwarranted state intervention, and as one respondent noted, are unlikely to understand the gravity of the situation because they have not experienced it. Darrell speaks of an "uncomfortable state of mind" that frames his encounters with law enforcement and suggests that the ability to "get over it"—a fairly common refrain from whites who do not experientially understand the breadth of the traffic stop—is unlikely to occur. The regularity of being stopped by law enforcement, evident in the remark "here we go again," becomes a part of his citizenship experience and a part of his relationship with the state. Darrell recognizes the effects of the panopticon as a way of restricting freedom thus reflecting Foucault's observation that hypersurveillance involves an awareness of the functioning of power for those under the panoptic effect. A key point includes Darrell's remarks on the "conscious and permanent visibility" Foucault sees as resulting from panopticonism. Darrell later describes how:

> individuals are still being enslaved mentally. That's the saddest part about it. Here you are—you've been unbound by physical shackles but you have mental shackles around you that are far worse than the ones you had physically.
>
> It's pretty hard. It affects the way we function in life as human beings. We have laws in place to. . . . I would say bind your mind with. Fear tactics. Control. To try to limit what freedom you have. I think that's what they really do and I wonder what is it going to take? Rodney King—people thought that was the Plymouth Rock of racial profiling. It's not! True enough, it's paramount in itself but it's not. There are so many other cases out there that aren't being heard. That aren't going to be heard because of fear. The fear. So many people of color in this nation and across the world worry about what if or what's next?

As in earlier references, Darrell makes an association with racial profiling processes and slavery, including how profiling processes are akin to "mental shackles" that influence everyday happenings. Racial profiling is rightfully seen as an extralegal mechanism for control by law enforcement. Darrell's comments illustrate the pervasiveness of racial oppression. He questions the ongoing process and wonders what other forms of oppression will rise up to meet him and his community.

Another respondent, Edgar, a Latino in his twenties with a college degree, remarks on the long lasting effects of racial profiling.

> It's already put, I guess that stain on me. That no matter now whenever I see PD they're not my friend. They're the enemy, the bad guys. I'm an educated person. I give everybody the benefit of the doubt but you see something, you feel something. You're always going to have that in you. Definitely when things keep happening the same way. You still feel that hurt feeling like you know what, maybe this is the way it is.

In this comment, Edgar's use of the term "stain" is indicative of the permanence of the panopticon experience as it is a reference to something that cannot be removed and is literally a physical mark. His narrative abounds with reference to the experiential aspect—the seeing, feeling, and repeated encounters—of profiling. He engages in credentialing ("I'm an educated person") and makes a point of saying that he offers the benefit of the doubt to people. Credentialing is a way to signal, in a classic criminology sense, commitment to society and thus engages the citizenship realm. Examination of the "benefit of the doubt" comment goes to the general critique of the vicarious experience variable in the current literature: People of color do not want to experience each encounter with white America as a racialized encounter and may downplay and deny racially active experiences.[13] Unlike some discourse that suggests minorities "play the race card," a running narrative from my respondents is of *not* wanting to consider encounters with the state as racialized encounters. Edgar's final comments illustrate the permanency of the racial profiling encounter ("You're always going to have that in you").

After relaying a particularly harrowing story about having a gun placed to his head by a police officer shortly after purchasing a soda and exiting a convenience store, another respondent, Nathan, a black male in his thirties with a graduate degree, framed the panopticon effect in the following way when asked why he considered a traumatic incident as racialized.

> Simply because it was not an isolated experience. I've experienced similar stuff over the years. Different name, different place or location. Just unusual stuff for no reason. . . . It's sort of in the subconscious that the combination of male, black, and young looking—put the three together and the image that the public, whether laity or professionals, has is a negative image. The three combined are just automatic prime suspects for just anything.
>
> At this stage in my life, I'm not surprised by it. Not that I agree with it but when it happens, I accept it as part of the black experience. I agree that there is something seriously wrong with it. . . . I've been dealing with that part of stuff for ages. It is a part of the experience. [My experience is] very minor compared to what the rest of the black experience, the rest of the black male experience, is like. I'd almost say it was nothing, a drop in the bucket.

Nathan's narrative illustrates how the regularity of profiling practices becomes normative for many people of color. His expression "automatic prime suspects" is informative as it indicates how the criminalization of young men of color is viewed under panopticonism. These instances also engage the double consciousness of DuBois because it reflects a struggle of identity. Nathan expresses awareness that his "black experience" of being criminalized is likely not as damaging as criminalization processes for less advantaged members of the black community. Concern for the collective is clearly a mark of citizenship engagement.

I asked Nathan if he discussed racial profiling concerns and resistance to racial profiling within his social network, as this process is fundamental to the vicarious experience and the lesson influences.

> Amongst peers, we do a little talking about that. . . .You don't have to like them but you have to respect them. That's with all authority figures—teachers, professors, any adults, anybody in authority. I don't make a generalization against the whole industry of law enforcement.
>
> As far as people of color, generally they are in positions of less power. The more power you have, the more favorable. The more power a person has overall then the lesser the consequences for challenging an unjust situation. If you're a person who doesn't have much power, then to challenge an unjust situation could have costs. The consequences would have been too severe. Just do what's best for the present.

In the above excerpt, Nathan indicates that his peer group doesn't include a lot of talk about police–minority relations. A later reference indicates his parents' strict influence shaped his "respect for authority" stance. He also makes a point to voice that he doesn't necessarily generalize his views of law enforcement to the whole of law enforcement. The latter part of the quote concerns issues of resistance and the body of knowledge that incorporates the lesson. While not making a direct reference to the lesson, his comments demonstrate awareness of the body of knowledge inherent to collective memory and how racial oppression operates. He suggests that resistance to racial oppression by the state needs to be shaped by the situation at hand ("do what's best for the present"), a staple of the ongoing communication across generations of color about how to handle encounters with the racial state.

Another respondent, Joseph, a black male in his forties with a graduate degree, mirrors Nathan's comments about the direct issue of power inherent in racial profiling: "it is an eliteness that these individuals have where they more or less think they can harass or pull over someone who may have the least power to do something about it. When I'm talking about power, I'm talking about money, I'm talking about power. I'm talking about a way of actually defending themselves." Joseph's narrative also brings to light how resistance strategies against power dynamics in the racial state may incorporate humor in renderings of the lesson: "[T]he comedian Richard Pryor told this story to thousands, millions of black people about an actual incident . . . but he made it into a joke. The officer asked him to get his driver's license and he said 'I am reaching in my pocket to get my driver's license." Of course, as he assumes the voice of Pryor, Joseph's speech slows to a very deliberate crawl as Pryor signals to the officer exactly what he is doing as a way to protect himself. Some thirty years later, comedian Dave Chappell uses similar "jokes," in his stand-up routines, indicating the slow progress on this front over the course of several decades.

Javier, a Latino in his late teens with some college education, relayed a story of how he and a group of friends—all Latinos—were singled out for law enforcement attention while nearby a group of white youth were scrutinized less harshly by the police. I asked Javier if and how his friends and family discuss the incident afterwards.

> Yeah. I think we were just being stupid like "Ah, hey, white people . . . " and this and that but mostly just cops in general. [How so?]
>
> I don't know. I guess that they make you feel really nervous when you're not really doing anything wrong. All the times when you'll be driving around, doing the speed limit and everything but the cop pulls beside you and be following you for a while. After so long, it's like—what did I do wrong? I start questioning myself like—"Oh my God, did I cut the guy off? What did I do?" Just like, from a child I always hated cops. I always thought they were just there to blame us for something.
>
> My dad always told me to act a little nicer with white police officers. I'll even see him. We'll get stopped for something. Of course I don't know why we'll get stopped. I guess it is my dad. He'll be in a nice neighborhood and he drives an old brown truck. I don't know what year it is but it is real beat up. He's a construction worker. His attitude changes quickly. He'll be real nice and his voice goes a little higher. The first thing is "Yes, sir." "No, sir." He'll be real nice. He's always told me to turn off the radio, make sure the car is a little clean. Of course, I'll be as polite as possible.

Javier's account shows how the panopticon effect may induce a sense of wrongdoing even when "you're not doing anything wrong." Under the watchful eye of the racial state, this operates as a function of power by keeping Javier self-aware and self-controlled. The young man also speaks about long-term alienation from law enforcement, likely brought on by the vicarious experiences of his father. Speaking of his father, elements of the lesson are evident in the backdrop of criminalization processes, particularly the extraordinary politeness that is used to deescalate potentially dangerous encounters with the state. The white racial frames[14] and white logic[15] that organize the racial order in the United States forces many whites and some people of color to compare the lesson to similar warnings spoken by white parents. The level of peril faced by young men of color in particular when they encounter the state is not comparable to that of whites, thus the lesson has an urgency other guidance does not.

Javier's narrative may be contextualized in a larger vicarious realm as well. As a youth, Javier is shaped by the experience of watching his father's mistreatment by the state. The current literature focus on vicarious experiences—because it is survey driven and comes from a "top-down" approach to examining racial profiling—misses this larger context. A vicarious experience is not only about shaping, in this case, Javier's view of the police as the relationship affects him alone. More critical analysis reveals that part of the alienation Javier experiences likely comes from how Javier sees the state deal with his father (and other family, friends, and strangers of color). He gains understanding of how the power held by the state is used against his father, whether he is able to articulate that consciously in his youthfulness or not. Finally, his comments point to the preparation communities of color engage in when dealing with the state. Feagin and Sikes discuss how people of color must expend energy dealing with—on numerous levels—issues concerning race that whites do not have to deal with.[16] Consequently, whites can use that energy for other concerns. Although whites also have a sense of being under the watchful eye of the law, the experience is different for many people of color because of the knowledge base of oppression and the accompanying concern for the collective that shapes their citizen–state relationship—the *two-ness* of which DuBois is concerned. I asked Javier how he deals with it all. His response goes to the permanence of the panopticon and the need to "live around it": "[I] know that I feel like it is there but it is something that is just never going to change. You just have to deal with it. Learn to live around it. No one really talks about it like that. I guess maybe in my family it's like it's never going to go away so just try your best to . . . stay away from . . . white cops."

Another respondent, Edgar, discusses the lesson and offers another dimension to the phenomenon.

> With my family, when we talk about law enforcement and just getting in trouble in general, usually they suggest just be submissive to it. Do whatever you have to do to get out of it, to get yourself out of that situation. You can make things worse. One simple action. One simple behavior or word or whatever. My family always says get yourself out of that situation.
>
> Hispanic people are usually religious. I'm not religious. I believe in God but I'm not as religious as my parents are. What they tell me, if you get in trouble, if one treats you a certain way, you know they're going to get judged. They'll get theirs. When they get theirs, it will be unfavorably. In a way it kind of gives peace to me. But I'm here right now. I want something done right now. I want something done right now. It's not. You've got to be rational. You've got to be rational. The best thing to do is just like I said. Do what you've got to do to get yourself out of that situation. It does give you comfort to know that they will be judged.

Again in this excerpt, very practical matters of survival comprise the core of the lesson. There is a concern that "one simple action" may be misconstrued by law enforcement and lead to a bad experience, thus demonstrating the very purpose-driven goal of the collective dialogue about law enforcement running through communities of color. Edgar's parents, in an attempt to help make sense of all of the caution they are encouraging in him, remind him that judgment day will come. Though he is somewhat resistant to biding his time until "judgment day" and wants "something done right now," ultimately Edgar finds some peace with his parents' belief that accountability will come.

Angela, a black female in her forties (no education given), provides another example of the omnipresence of the panopticon effect. She describes a riot in her neighborhood following an arrest of a young man many in her community felt was unjustified. I asked her why the community reacted so strongly and she quickly goes into the constant patrolling and monitoring characteristic of the panopticon effect.

> They beat him. . . . Sometimes it might just be a reaction they see you with. When they pull up they might see you with your hands in your pockets at the wrong time. There's really not a right way or a wrong way to do that over here. If you see an officer come around this corner and say I'm coming out of this parking lot, I might just so happen to put my hand in my pocket walking to my door. They quickly assume and pull over and pull up in here and say "I saw you stick your hands in your pocket." But when they get here, you don't have nothing but your keys and change. They don't even apologize. They just assume. There's always an assumption!

> K: So they're thinking that you're putting something away—like a bag?

> A: Yeah. All the time. When they come, it's like there's never no good person over here. They want to say everybody over here is the same. We all sell, we all, you know. It's like everybody's judged by the same color.

In the above excerpt, Angela points to the criminalization that occurs in her community and how everyday activities are monitored and suspected. Her comments point out the ongoing nature of the panopticon. The panopticon effect—this assumption of guilt that Angela and her community must negotiate daily—creates alienating relations with the state. Dominant group members are largely protected from developing similar alienating relations with the state.[17] I asked Angela to expand on the effects of these criminalizing experiences.

> When I see it, it makes me angry because to me it's not showing leadership. To me I feel like where I was raised, the police officers were the ones that carried the number one leadership for anybody. Of what I've seen and experienced with some of these police officers over here, be no more than what we have to deal with ourselves out here as a pedestrian. You could see some of them come over here where it's like I already have a bad attitude, and

some of them will tell us that—"Look, I've had a long, bad day, and you're just urking my nerves or pissing me the hell off." You might come to a place where you say, ok, "Can I speak to your superiors so that we won't get into it further and let your superior make a decision about you treating me like this or what." "Call my goddamn superior! I don't give a damn."

K: Earlier you were saying that when the police officer was really giving you a hard time, you went to Internal Affairs. It seemed like that did something?

A: Well, it quieted down. I never saw the officer again. . . . The way I was raising my children, I voiced that opinion to them a lot. If something comes up with a police officer, and they feel like they can't talk to that police officer, they have a right to ask for their superior. Because everybody has a boss. That's what I teach them.

Regarding vicarious experience and the lesson, Angela indicates that her view of law enforcement was a relatively positive one when she was growing up. The experiential effect of racial oppression by law enforcement changed her relationship with the state. Contrary to the underlying public domain discourse that suggests communities of color perpetuate conflict themselves and unquestioningly adopt negative (and unfounded) views of law enforcement, the communications she received as a young person were not wholly detrimental to her view of the police. It was the experiential nature of her relations with the police that was likely most influential. Angela refers to one incident in which she invoked the citizenship realm and made an official complaint about police mistreatment. In this context, the lesson is evident as she discusses the teachings she passes on to her children (and likely to others as she was a community activist). The lesson, as presented here, is clearly a way to support people of color in the ways of a racial state, specifically by engaging due rights to hold the state accountable.

The vicarious experience is not about passively adopting the views of others who have had negative experiences with the state. Because vicarious experience is considered an important explanatory factor by many of the current racial profiling researchers, it is crucial to deconstruct its parts to comprehend what it is about the process that makes it so influential. The critical and in-depth analysis of vicariousness in the current examination illustrates how it is a reminder that the personal is political.[18] Vicariousness, when contextualized within an understanding of how the lesson operates for communities of color, is a mechanism to directly impact the lives of people of color. The lesson in this instance clearly indicates it is about how to negotiate citizenship. As such, it reflects as well DuBois's argument that people of color have insight about the world emergent from racial oppression. Because of white racial frame and white logic orientations, mainstream research's focus on vicarious experience can only superficially tap into the deeper meanings of this "imagined participation" quality of vicariousness.

Another respondent, Cristina, a Latina in her twenties with a high school education, offers a rendering of the reconciliation of somewhat positive images of law enforcement she had as a child and images and experiences she has as an adult. She also remarks on the complexities of police–minority relations.

> I do think sometimes they take matters into their own hands. That stuff shouldn't occur because you bring up kids to think "Oh, the police are good people. They're here to take care of you and to watch over you, here to protect you." Then when the kids see the police beating on people on TV, what do you think? You're just confusing them like any other thing. In a way I think it depends on how you respond to the police because there's no need to think you're always right. Sometimes you have to accept that you're wrong or that the person is a suspect or something. Sometimes they're wrong also. It's hard to tell. There's so many people that they come across that are bad people and they have to do their job.

Kimberly, a black female in her forties with a graduate degree, relays a story about a particularly tense encounter she had with law enforcement. The incident, as with other respondents, was described in great detail and indicates the staying power of these watershed events in people's lives. I asked if and how she discussed the incident with family and friends.

> I guess in a sense in going back and talking about this to people . . . when I talk to people of color and people in my family, yeah, they have a tendency to downplay it because it is something that is so prevalent, I guess, that blacks are being discriminated against. It's just like another occurrence. But for me, I haven't experienced a lot of personal experience with racism and those types of things. When I see, when it affects me, it affects me tremendously. I automatically realize what's going on, you know?

Family and friends may tend to downplay racializing and criminalizing events because of the everydayness of these and other forms of racial oppression. It may be a pick-your-battle form of resistance, with some instances of oppression left relatively unaddressed outside of the critical consciousness described by DuBois. The everydayness of the events, though not unexpected in a racial state, are still highly meaningful and as we see with Kimberly, especially disconcerting in cases where someone feels he or she has not experienced "a lot" of racial discrimination. Hence, the vicarious experiences that the current literature concentrates on are likely meaningful for their respondents because of the accompanying *experiential* events that back them up. When family and friends discuss these events, the effect is not that they *create* a racialized sense among each other (an underlying supposition in the current literature), the effect that is created is one of support of their collective understanding of racial oppression and its myriad manifestations. Kimberly expands on the concerns of the lesson and the necessity of having to worry about getting oneself out of the situation in the excerpt below.

> I think that that's what people in my social networks and stuff [think] . . . yeah. When you're pulled over by the police, hey—just sit there, wait to hear what he has to say, answer questions. Just cooperate. Even though my perspective about police officers may have changed, I still am someone who believes in respecting other people. So if a police officer approaches me and they are respectful of me, I am also respectful. At the same time I'm not going to allow them to talk to me in a degrading manner without responding to that. . . . But for the most part, I've heard, in talking in general with people, that's what they tell you. Just pull over and cooperate. I think a lot of people think that the police can do anything to you and justify it and get away with it. So that's definitely, for the most part, the nature of the conversation. Very cooperative.

Prompted by her comment above, I asked Kimberly how she was changed by her experience.

> Yeah, I am very critical of the police. When I see things on TV when police are involved, I automatically question whether the police did something to provoke. I know that is not the case in all situations. But this sense of abuse of power. I think one of the reasons I'm in the field I am in is because I have an inherent want to try to help people who are disadvantaged and not empowered. I think it raised for me to experience that so— frontline-ish—it just, yeah. It did something to me to be in that position, to be that person. To . . . to be made to feel so . . . devalued. You know, personally.

The encounter with the police that Kimberly describes changed her relationship with the state yet she does not make unqualified assumptions about every citizen–state encounter gone wrong. She reflects on how the encounter was motivating in her work with issues of justice. Kimberly's use of the warfare discourse ("to experience that so—frontline-ish"), as earlier with Darrell, is significant and goes to the power dynamic inherent in racialization and criminalization processes. She discusses the panoptic effect of the racialized surveillance and more directly addresses vicarious experiences in the continuation below.

> It stays with you. It stayed with me because it was like one of the first times. I heard a whole bunch of stories. My parents talked about stories and how people, just to their face, kind of belittled them or tried. I had never experienced

> that. So for one, it stays with me because it was something out of my regular experience. Two because you see it. You see it everywhere. You see it on TV. You hear people talking about it. And the fact that it is not going away. It's here! It bothers me because it is so structural it's hard to see how to make any changes. You can do all the things, all the things society says is valued yet still based on skin color, you can be devalued. Yeah, it makes me angry. It makes me extremely angry.
>
> I feel like a lot of years, I bought into the system. I bought into the system of if you work hard, if you achieve this education, if you do this, whatever, that somehow it will kind of lessen the bad experiences. For a long time, I used to think that. I used to believe that people who—I have to say blacks because that is my experience—who didn't achieve, that was because they just didn't try. Oh, there was a lot of "white man this . . . white man that." That's what I heard a lot. That experience with that police officer and shortly thereafter was the Rodney King incident. When I saw the Rodney King incident, that made me realize that blacks in America can be treated *however*, and the world can see it and nobody will say that it is wrong. I was so angry that I was almost anti-America to a certain point. I didn't believe anything about America. That is when I started my quest, somehow, to try to make a difference.

Kimberly's narrative is informative because it shows how she rejected some of the information she was receiving about how race operated in the United States prior to her own damaging encounter with the state. This is contrary to the vicarious experience discourse suggesting that those without their own personal experiences adopt (negative) views of law enforcement unquestioningly. Although Kimberly acknowledges that the event was outside of her normal experience, the narrative that follows frames her experience within the broader collective experience people of color have within a racial state. She explains how she used to believe some people of color were exaggerating experiences of inequality. Kimberly understands the contradiction between being criminalized yet having other identities that show commitment to society ("You can do all the things . . . society says is valued yet still based on skin color, you can be devalued"). She makes a direct reference to a break from citizenship ("I didn't believe anything about America") and how the experiential nature of her encounter and the following outrage over the Rodney King beating outweighed her earlier conceptions of how racial inequality occurred. Finally, Kimberly's narrative demonstrates how these experiences with the state can lead to resistance to the oppression, including efforts at reform. The denial of full citizenship treatment and Kimberly's consciousness that this occurred because of her racial status provides another example of DuBois's conceptions of self-identity, imposed identity, and the ensuing struggles that result.

Another dimension where the panopticon effect, the lesson, and vicarious experience concepts show themselves is evident in the following narrative from Kimberly. She expands on how her relationship with the state changed following her racial profiling encounter. As with Darrell, another respondent, Kimberly reflects on the racialized traffic stop, its oppressive qualities and slavery. Her comments point to the complexity of racial oppression and the various mechanisms and dimensions of awareness and resistance. Kimberly's association of her experiences in understanding racial profiling with slavery also reflects the linkages between the past and the present that comprise collective memory, the broader realm of the lesson.

> I recall having told people that "Oh, it doesn't have anything to do with the white people. You just don't want to try." I recall telling people that. . . . I mean I had so bought into the system. I think when I realized that, when I was so disillusioned that I had bought into it—I had assimilated so much—that I was sounding, probably to blacks, I was sounding just like white America. It reminded me so much [of] back in slavery. The female, the mother, or the wife would often times have to act like the liaison with her husband out in the field and how the master treated him. She would have to kind of say "Oh, master is ok." So it was almost giving some legitimacy to what was happening to them. I felt that. I felt so betrayed. Disillusioned in a sense that I went completely over to the totally opposite end. I would say as time has gone by and I've gotten older and I've learned more, I'm learning to get back toward the middle where I recognize who I am and I recognize what America stands for. I don't see all white people as representing that. I'm on an even keel where I can determine, I can say what my experiences are without necessarily making a generalization about everybody in the group.

In this excerpt, Kimberly explains how she adopted some of the main tenets of white supremacy ideology, what Bonilla-Silva has labeled as abstract liberalism.[19] In this framework, whites use the American creed to explain their position in the social order and attribute "troubles" with communities of color as a consequence of their not working as hard. Nowhere in the discourse is there mention that whiteness or racial minority status is explanatory to the social order. Because this ideology is rampant in the public discourse and ingrained in our everyday teachings of what it means to be an American, even some people of color adopt its frameworks.

Kimberly discusses how recognition of her assimilation was "disillusioning." Like Darrell in earlier references, she makes a connection between racializing and criminalizing processes of the state in contemporary times and slavery. Likely, articulating this connection is not taken lightly by either respondent. Her discussion of it makes clear that it is something she has considered and related to in other contexts.

Pam, a black woman in her thirties with a college degree, also discusses the lesson and vicarious experience link. Her experience with the criminal justice system does validate the vicarious experience premise in a sense that most of the interview centered on her brother's experience in the criminal justice system. I asked her if and how she discussed issues of racial and ethnic status with family and friends.

> Well, this one comment I would hear from time to time. I was raised up in a low economic area and one thing they would always say is you better watch your back. You better be careful as it relates to getting in trouble because once you get in trouble, because of who you are and where you live, you're just going to be doomed. They would say you are going to be stuck. They don't care about you. You will be treated differently because of who you are. Black—just who you are. They would always say that, you would hear that throughout. You see it on TV. You see it with the Rodney King case, you know, just because of who he was. They would say that. It was kind of hard for me to believe at some points.

In this excerpt, collective voices of concern exposed Pam to a view of a race-based criminal justice system, with the Rodney King beating and other media influences collaborating some of these earlier views. Yet Pam's final comment about doubts she had on the input she was receiving regarding how race operated in the criminal justice system suggests that these vicarious experiences, again, are not passively adopted by people of color.

Another narrative that engages this sense of doubt about the realities of the panopticon emerges from Manuel, a Latino in his thirties with an associate's degree. Manuel introduces the idea that the panopticon effect works as a reciprocal process. Unique in his response, Manuel's view is likely influenced by the time he spent in prison. Over the course of the interview, he made several references to the fact that he had a prison record and thus believed the police were somewhat justified in targeting him for law enforcement after his release. However, he clearly struggled to reconcile those rationalizations with the rehabilitation he enjoyed in prison, specifically the education he received, and with his continued efforts in education and success in holding down a good job. In the excerpt below, I asked Manuel how he explained the more negative levels of support for the police from people of color.

> I think it works both ways. If they're looking at us, if they're trying—"Oh, there's some blacks over there . . . or some Hispanics, we better watch 'em. . . ." I think every time a cop pops up, I'm thinking I better watch out because he could [do something]. I do that a lot. I could be driving down the road and I'm like—"Ah man, here come the cops." See how I got an attitude already toward them? I didn't even do nothing.

> Because of racial profiling. That's why I say it kind of works both ways. If they're looking at us like that already and thinking negative, well it works the other way around too. When they pop up, in my mind they're either going to target me, harass me, hassle me, mess with me. There could be some other people there too but I would stick out.

In this excerpt, Foucault's sense of how the power of panopticonism becomes instilled in the individual (and collective) is evident. Manuel internalizes the all-seeing eye of the state and makes a link between the profiling practices of the state and his own automatic sense that he is a special target for the state. This reciprocation results in alienation. As Foucault argues, disciplinary power from the state is:[20]

> exercised through its invisibility; at the same time it imposes on those whom it subjects a principle of compulsory visibility. In discipline, it is the subjects who have to be seen. Their visibility assures the hold of the power that is exercised over them. It is the fact of being constantly seen, of being able always to be seen, that maintains the disciplined individual in his subjection. And the examination is the technique by which power, instead of emitting the signs of its potency, instead of imposing its mark on its subjects, holds them in a mechanism of objectification.

While Manuel's comments point to a reciprocal quality of racial profiling, Victor, a Latino in his midtwenties with some college, introduces yet another dimension—the importance of social space in racial profiling processes. Social space restrictions, the *who belongs where* reality that shapes American neighborhoods (a consequence of racialized historical and contemporary practices) is a defining social control mechanism of a racial state. In the following excerpt, Victor is responding to my inquiry about the different levels of support for police across racial and ethnic groups.

> Because they spend more time in our neighborhoods. They're looking at us a lot. I will see one police officer in Queen's Crossing [a wealthy and white area of the city]. Maybe it's because they have security guards. Maybe not. But most of the crimes, I agree, happen in black neighborhoods, Hispanic neighborhoods. That's where you see most of the police officers. Looking. You see one, you see three more coming right behind you. That's why a lot of us feel that way. It's like you can't even go outside and take out the trash without seeing one.
>
> My mom used to say, "if the shoe fits, wear it." If you're guilty about it, if you're guilty of something, they're going to come get you. But then if you're not and you're still being put into that box with everybody else, that's when those feelings come about.

> K: Almost like the regularity of seeing the police in your neighborhood isn't giving you a sense of security . . . ?

> M: Absolutely not. Why do I need the police officers to make me feel secure? For us, it's more a feeling of being supervised, of being looked down upon . . . of the need for the police officers needing to be there on a regular basis. You don't see that on the south side of town.

A common rationalization to explain disproportionate traffic stops across racial and ethnic groups concerns the allocation of law enforcement resources to "high crime" areas, commonly referred to as the "deployment" argument. If law enforcement is primarily allocated to areas with a large population of low socioeconomic and racial minority status residents—often those communities designated as high crime areas—the reasoning is that it *makes sense* that people of color will be subjected to more attention from the police due to where they live. This is a major argument in justifications for racial profiling. While the practice will ensure arrests for particular types of crime, it also may account for the lack of monitoring of other social spaces where different types of crime, like white-color crime, occur.

Victor's narrative engages, to an extent, this rationale. His remarks also point out how the patrolling and monitoring of minority space weighs heavy on his mind. He makes reference to what I call the "guilt factor." In some discussions of racial profiling, people of color may state that there is nothing problematic about being pulled over by the police if indeed the person of color made a traffic infraction. Victor's mother's comment goes to this idea ("if the shoe fits, wear it"). The rationalization is complicated by Victor's awareness that people of color who engage in crime, because they are scrutinized to a larger degree than whites, are more likely to wind up in the system ("if you're guilty about something, they're going to come get you"). This connection becomes clearer in the second part of the quote when he brings up the surveillance that permeates his community ("it's more of a feeling of being supervised"), and how the white space of the south side of town is not surveilled to a similar degree.

The majority of respondents were critical in their assessments of how social space was regulated along racial and ethnic lines. For example, Mary, a black woman in her eighties with a graduate degree, expresses frustration with the state when I asked her why she thought she was stopped by the police on a recent occasion:

> Because I was black and I was driving a nice car. I didn't think it was any of his business where I was going. "Where are you going?" I haven't had that much contact with police anyway but it just really . . . made me feel bad. Here I am an old lady, a private citizen, not speeding, not breaking any laws. To be pulled over and asked "Where are you going?" . . . You can't judge a book by its cover. I've been around people who looked like they didn't have a dime and they pull out a roll that would choke a horse.

The "where are you going?" comment, particularly for a black woman in her eighties who experienced legal segregation for many years, is an affront to the liberties of citizenship she identifies with, as it suggests certain space is off limits to her. Her narrative also points to the intersection of race and class in these processes.

Alberto, a Latino in his midfifties with some college, engaged a more conservative view of the criminalization of social space. The argument is very much a part of the discourse explaining racial minority overrepresentation in the criminal justice system. After some initial discussion of the topic, I introduced the two main views of the issue, including the rational discrimination argument engaged in part of Victor's (and Alberto's) narrative and the argument that generalizations about social space cut a wide swath across neighborhoods that actually contain a large majority of law-abiding citizens.

> Well, it can be a little bit of both, I guess. You can get officers that are prejudiced and that's the only way they can demonstrate power, that they have power over others and going at the weakest links which are the minorities because they don't have the money to defend themselves. They're found in the neighborhoods and housing areas that are more riddled with crime because of their economic situation. Because of this they raise a red flag which brings attention to them from the police because they are in these areas. They are going to get more attention because they are in the areas that are more riddled with crime. So, whoever is there, which is usually the poor and minorities, they're the ones that are going to get the attention from the police and get arrested more often.
>
> It probably does happen because the officers get used to arresting minorities because they're the ones that are found where the trouble's at. They're the ones who they control in the troubled areas. So then they start thinking they got to be looking for minorities all of the time. Because they are the ones being arrested. They're the ones that are involved with the police. Unless, uh . . . the people that have the money are not going to be found in those places most of the time unless they go by just to buy drugs or whatever. But they're going to be in better neighborhoods and the police are not going to be patrolling those neighborhoods if there is nobody outside—like on the corners—like there are in the poor areas.

Alberto's narrative shows a complex view of police–minority relations. His focus on social space was rationalized because of the emphasis on street crime that defines criminal justice orientations in the United States. The panoptic focus on minority space is commonsensical to Alberto. However, he recognizes the crime that occurs in "better neighborhoods" is not monitored and surveilled similarly. Later, Alberto engages the idea that "all it takes is one or two to give a neighborhood a bad name. It's very few the ones that are causing the problems."

Though not directly a traffic stop encounter, Jerome, a black male in his forties with a college degree and a former police officer, relayed an account of how he was mistaken for a burglar suspect by a police officer as he walked outside of his home in a predominantly white neighborhood (thus qualifying as a criminalizing *raced* encounter with the state). In the first few seconds of the encounter, the officer unsnapped his holster, indicating potential use of lethal force. I asked Jerome if he could discuss why he thought the life-threatening incident was racialized.

> Well, I go on previous experiences too. I want all of your audience to know, I don't try to act like there's a problem. I just be aware of it in the back of my mind. It says "Warning warning, watch out." What I did was just walk out there. I wasn't mad. I was very calm. I was thinking about baby poop [a new father, Jerome was carrying out two large trash bags of dirty baby diapers when he was approached]. I'm thinking about the next day. I teach. I'm thinking about my next day's lesson plan, what particular kid was giving me problems. I had no problem with no police. I was just there, had a hoagie sandwich waiting for me and a big old nice glass of Kool-Aid. That's what my mind was on—eating! Very calm. But when he came out and shined the big light in my face, I knew there was going to be trouble. He already had me guilty. From the tone of his voice to his mannerisms to the way he came out at me on my property and asking me "Did I live here?" He's telling me "You don't belong, sir. You don't belong here."

Jerome provides a unique perspective in that he was once a police officer and, from an earlier reference, believes he has experienced racial profiling dozens of times over the course of his life. He is concerned that readers of the present study understand that he does not assume there will be racial issues with law enforcement when he encounters them. However, he is intimately aware that he needs to be prepared in case something does arise. The statement about not making a problem out of every encounter goes to the public discourse surrounding the vicarious experience. Part of the underlying implication with vicarious experience is that communities of color themselves *create* problems with law enforcement by their ongoing discussion in the community about historical racial oppression. Jerome, perhaps because of his law enforcement background and familiarity with the police and public discourse on the subject, quickly wants to dismiss the notion that his *expectation* of racial oppression is the real problem in the encounter. As an act of resistance, this points to Collins's concern with self-definition and valuation of oppressive encounters. The detailed account of his thoughts at the time point to the everydayness of racial profiling processes. His point is to show how criminalization crashes in on everyday life and citizenship status may be revoked without warning.

Jerome's narrative is important in part because it provides another example of the salience of social space in racial profiling processes. The panopticon effect includes concerns about the prohibition and management of social space as some areas may produce a more intense panopticon experience. For example, one respondent stated how he "knew where not to drive" in the town to which he had recently moved. In Jerome's excerpt, the criminalizing effect of the panopticon is clear, as is the spatial restraint ("He's telling me 'You don't belong, sir'"). These notions of having freedom in social space coincide with Darrell's earlier concept of "mental freedom," with both supporting the citizen–minority dichotomy of concern to DuBois.

Later, Jerome again imparts the idea that people of color don't necessarily assume an adversarial stance with the state but have collectively learned to go into encounters with the state with some apprehension. The apprehension is a result of the experiential and collective lessons in communities of color.

> I'm sorry, I get a little emotional, you know, talking about things like that. It brings up the dread. It makes me kind of bitter. No, I don't have a chip on my shoulder but it makes you feel like, hey, I'm being treated like that in 2005. It just kind of makes you aware of it. Every time a cop stops you, you're not paranoid, but you're like—am I going to get a good cop? Am I going to get a bad cop? Am I going to get somebody who is understanding to minorities?

Because of the enormity of his experience with racial profiling, I was very interested in if and how he shared these experiences among his family and friends.

> I'm always guided by my family. African American guys pass it on. Men pass it on how the police treat them. Older guys told me but I was always reluctant because I lived in the quote "white society." I kept always telling my black friends "Ah, that don't happen." Then whoa whoa whoa. Had to admit it. I was in denial. That's wrong. I was in denial and I didn't think it could be.
>
> As African Americans, you've got to be real calm. Sometimes you've got to bite your tongue to really not get pissed off and go to jail. Sometimes you're pissed off. African Americans are pissed off because we didn't have a picture that we would get treated like that in today's society. It's 2005. As an African American, the mindset is you don't want to get treated that way and you still get treated that way—like it's back in the 60s. We haven't overcome anything! It's still out there.
>
> Those things have happened to me. It makes you wiser. It makes you conservative. It makes you aware of your surroundings. It makes you, not paranoid, but if the cops stop you, you better be really sharp and pay attention to everything he says. Make sure you take some notes emotionally—notes

> about what is going on. Be sharp on your game. Whatever you've got to do, that's what you have to do. I've been through that and managed to obtain a college degree, I've managed to teach school for twenty-two years. I've managed to be a productive citizen in our society even though there's negativity towards African Americans in this world. I'm going to live my life. I'm going to live my life to the fullest.

Initially, Jerome was reluctant to adopt the admonitions of his elders. He attributes this to his experience living in "white society" and being in "denial." Jerome expresses a main tenet of the lesson—remain calm in encounters with law enforcement. This aspect of the lesson has historical roots in group survival strategies of communities of color and remains relevant today. Yet, in an example of how the lesson may shape resistance strategies, Jerome puts a positive spin on how having to remain constantly mindful of oppression signals wisdom.

Jason, a black male in his midthirties with an associate's degree, offered two intricately detailed accounts of specific racial profiling incidents he experienced. As with Jerome and others, he engages the idea that the panopticon effect is part of his experience as a black male—the *two-ness* to which DuBois refers—and discussed as such in his community. The following is his response to my question about how he deals with these encounters by the state.

> I think growing up, I've been taught this is something that is going to happen to you. You are going to make the situation worse if you get angry or you act suspicious. In both of those situations, I can remember being a little bit aggravated or ticked off but at the same time, because of what my parents taught me, you just don't want to make the situation any worse. If you argue with the officer, if you show any type of anger or aggression, it's just going to escalate the situation. I can definitely remember, when we were in Massachusetts, me and my friend, once he let us go we were discussing where we were in the line of cars [a reference to the officer's rationale for stopping him]. Of course we came to the deduction that we were not at that time the lead car. That was just an excuse that he was making. We did ride on for about a half hour just talking about how terrible that is. It does make you angry.
>
> As a race I think that is the idea or the feeling that we have from law enforcement—that we're suspicious because we're African American. We have to be up to something. If they stop us then it's going to lead to some type of bust. It is aggravating. It can be very aggravating. Sad to say that it is a part of life that as a race we teach our young men that "Hey—this is going to happen to you and you better be prepared for it. It's going to happen. Not that it might happen, but that it is going to happen sooner or later. You're going to get stopped and you won't have to be doing anything but crossing the street. You're going to get stopped and you're going to get questioned." That's just life. We just learn to accept it as part of our interaction with law enforcement.

In this excerpt, Jason makes reference to the lesson and the underlying presence of the panopticon in his experience as a black male ("this is something that is going to happen to you"). As with other respondents, the impetus for passing on the information isn't directed at perpetuating negative relations among communities of color and the state but clearly about very practical issues of survival. The panoptic experience is evident in his repeated remarks about constant surveillance being "a part of life" and the need to accept it as part of interactions with the state. Because Jason was adamant about the role of the lesson in the minority experience, I asked him to discuss the implications of some of the discourse surrounding the vicarious experience—specifically the idea that communities of color reproduce racial conflict in relations with the state themselves because they carry on this collective dialogue.

> I think that it's easy for white America to say that if minorities, African Americans, stop talking about these incidents, then maybe they wouldn't happen so much. It's part of our life, whether we talk about it or not. These are incidents that are going on. So to speak, if you don't talk about the rain, the rain is still gonna come down. It's just a force of nature. This is just something that we have to deal with. I'm not sure who did it but I remember some type of study on the police. . . . The alarming thing out of that study was that white America has no concept or no idea of what it's like to whenever you see a police officer, to know that they are watching you. All of the African American college students said that they were stopped and questioned. It just speaks so much to the fact that if you're an African American male between the age of fifteen and thirty, let's say, you're going to get stopped from time to time. That's just a fact of life. If we stop talking about it, I guarantee that it is still going to occur. Our not talking about it is not going to change the way law enforcement do their business or this notion that we have to be up to something.

Jason's narrative really goes to the heart of the issue with the vicarious experience discourse in the current literature and more generally in the public discourse. Though this discourse is underlying and subtle, I argue that it becomes legitimate in the mainstream criminology community because it engages the *playing the race card* discourse inherent to both public and academic arenas when examining racial and ethnic relations.

Veon, a black female in her forties with a high school education, focused most of her narrative on the death of her son while in police custody. While not specifically addressing the issue of racialized traffic stops, it does go to the more general impact of racial and ethnic status in the criminal justice system. Veon's son was pulled over by the police and ingested a quantity of crack cocaine to avoid getting caught possessing the illegal substance. According to Veon, his girlfriend who was a passenger in the car told the police that he had swallowed the drug and would require medical attention. The police ignored repeated requests for medical aid even once Veon's son began to experience health problems. He was eventually taken to the hospital where he died.

> Regardless of what he did, he was still my child. I just don't understand why the system is so messed up. We have so many people who have been abused and we can't explain why the system can do us like that. If someone out there can help us, I wish they could. I'm a mother praying for help. I hope we find a solution for this to help someone else. I don't want another mother to go through this. I'm still dealing with losing my son. It's not about the money or anything, it was just about justice. The system is corrupt.
>
> To me they put my son in a cage, felt like he wasn't nobody, and just put him in the cage to die. He was a son, a father, a brother and he was human. Me myself, I just felt like they were going to do justice and everything. I don't speak out like this . . . but they are so corrupt.

> K: Did you have a good sense of the system?
>
> V: Oh yes I did! Yes. This right here, it made me know that they're wrong, they're crooked. There's something wrong! My son is not the only one.

Veon's account provides another example of the experiential quality of racial oppression. Prior to this tragic incident, Veon's view of the system was characterized by "justice." The break from a belief in the system that occurred with Veon's experience demonstrates how influential the experiential quality of racial oppression is to understanding views of justice.

Hector, a Latino in his forties with a high school education and vocational training, explains how his numerous experiences with law enforcement, and the everydayness of it, gives him a sense of being disenfranchised as a citizen of the United States, a reference clearly in the framework of DuBois's concern with reconciling "American" and racial minority identity. I interviewed Hector at his barber shop and also engaged a young man in the shop, Michael, a Latino in his twenties with some college education, on a number of concerns about racial profiling.

> Hector: It discourages me to have to deal with especially the police. I have to worry about every time I go to the store—am I going to be pulled over? Harassed? I'm even afraid to call the police if something happens to my house. If I have problems at my business, I usually don't call the police because I'm afraid they're going to get the wrong idea. Like if I have a problem here at the shop, I don't call them so I won't have to deal with it. I'm not friendly with them. When I was growing up, I felt that police officers were to be trusted and to be obeyed. Now I'm distrustful of them.
>
> Michael: Some people say just cooperate even though the cops are wrong and you know your rights. Cooperate with them. The majority of people I know would say something like that. If they get in trouble for something

they didn't do, let the cops say what they have to say. Let them do what they have to do so they can go about their business. The majority of time it is shut up, not say nothing, agree with whatever he says, do whatever he says.

Hector: Yeah, that's the way my parents are too. They're from the old school. Whatever the police tell you, you just do it. The police here are brought up that way—to be distrustful of Hispanics and blacks and to always think that they sell drugs, run around with guns and knives and that we're not decent people. We are. We're just normal like everyone else.

There's some good people in this neighborhood. Good people who have grown up to become attorneys, doctors and they come back to visit their mom and dad and are surprised by the way they're treated. Welcome to the real world! I don't know about the Civil Rights Act. If Martin Luther King would come back from the grave, I think he'd say "Oh well. . . ."

In these excerpts, Hector shares that he had positive views of the police as a young person but later encounters taught him to be "distrustful" of law enforcement. Michael picks up on this theme and extends it to the lesson. This easy segue comes from his connection with not trusting law enforcement and having his community give guidance on how to approach encounters with law enforcement. Again, while whites are also instructed to respond to law enforcement direction and the like, the experience is different for communities of color due to historical and contemporary realities. Hector's support of Michael's remarks is contextualized within the panopticon effect ("police are brought up to . . . always think that they sell drugs. . . .") and an underlying concern with why his community is scrutinized. The final comment is meaningful as it suggests that even achievement of high socioeconomic status is not an insulating factor for people of color, an insight that is supported in the current study in contrast to other work[21] that demonstrates the expected protective character of high socioeconomic status in the criminal justice system.

In the following narrative, Carlos, a Latino in his early thirties with a graduate degree, describes his experiences with the lesson.

The sad part is that in my family there was, I don't carry this with me, contrary to what you believe, my family completely distrusts the police. They've been hurt by them, physically, beat up. When I was 16, 17 they'd try to put this on me and I completely reject it. They view me as the educated one—"He goes to college so he's exempt from that." The funny part, the ironic part, is that I'm not. I'm not exempt from that because I'm educated because you cannot show your education on your car. If you could I probably would. You know, just like those little stickers they have—"I support the Sheriff's Department." Get that, get that! You're fine. It works. It's the same thing, if I could say "I'm on your side" somehow on my car, but I'm not. I'm not. Those days, they're over. They were done when I was in high school. Now

> that I'm a grown man, an adult, I distrust the police the way my father and my grandfather told me. But I would never project that. I talk to young men and they say this and I say "Come on man. . . ." I would never kind of disclose how I really feel, that would be unprofessional. If you could hear their stories, young men, black and Hispanic, it's unbelievable. And they don't have a voice. I do. We have voices. [Some] Young men don't.

Similar to other narratives, Carlos points out that he was not easily swayed by family discussions about law enforcement, saying he "completely reject[ed] it" as a young man. As with Hector, there is a discussion of how socioeconomic status is not protective of undue state interference ("you cannot show your education on your car"). His distrust of the police comes as a result of experience with law enforcement and is not merely an adoption of his family's view of the police. A community organizer who works with young Latino fathers, Carlos states that in respect for his position he makes a conscious effort not to impose his views of the state on the young people with whom he works.

Later, Carlos remarks on the consequences of the panopticon and its focus on communities of color.

> He's a good kid . . . who got pulled over at the wrong time and just snaps—he's branded as a juvenile or a trouble maker. Or a cop doing this or that or whatever just because of that single act. That's it. He's branded for life. I mean the significance of that—of racial profiling—is just the fact that one incident can really affect a person for the rest of his life. Maybe not bringing it out in the open like we are but constantly day after day when you see that cop car. We don't see that's our friendly neighbor.
>
> . . . It's almost like we've been given this fairy tale that cops are the good guys. The cop standing there, you know, helping old ladies—whatever. This is reality. This is the way it really is. Sure, you may be educated, you may hear about it on TV, you may read about it but until you experience it—you're like "Oh shoot." . . . That's the feeling you get in your gut. It's a loss of innocence. This is reality. This is the way your life is going to be. You're a Hispanic male—get used to it.

Carlos reflects on the detrimental effects of the panopticon not only in its lingering and consistent effects but in how racial profiling processes act as potential entree into the criminal justice system. He comments on how the role of the police officer presented in society is vastly different than the role many people of color are subjected to in their everyday encounters. He continues this line of concern with another reference to the everydayness of racialization and criminalization processes and how racial profiling encounters with the state are watershed moments ("a loss of innocence") that men of color must get used to. Later, he refers to his experiences as "like constantly being under a microscope."

Jesse, a Latino in his early twenties with some college education, offers a unique analysis of his experiences with racial profiling. In the following excerpt, he is responding to my question about definitions and conceptions of the term racial profiling.

> Racial profiling? What I think about is authority figures acting on stereotypes. It's funny, sometimes we'll go out driving and I'll actually feel safer when there are white people in the car. I will actually feel like, ok pull me over, there's white people in the car. Now that I think about it, I've actually never been pulled over with a white person in the car. I didn't think about that until right now.

The narrative is informative because it provides the flip side of the panopticon experience. For Jesse, a white partner acts as a buffer between him and the state. There is an implied concern that not only is the likelihood of getting stopped lessened when a white person is in the vehicle but that even if there is a stop, it has less potential to end up badly. The panopticon effect—an awareness of state surveillance and the inherent power dynamic that accompanies it—is muted by the presence of the white partner. As he continues, Jesse connects racial profiling by the police to larger racist systems shaping society.

> It's not just the police. It's also just society itself. For instance, when that lady drowned her two kids in the pool by locking them in her car and killed her two sons. What was she saying? A black guy. Yeah, we just feed the whole frenzy here. The runaway bride. She said a Mexican kidnapped her in a painter's van. That's what they do! You never quite hear of a minority kid that goes missing. You hear of white kids that go missing. It's not just the cops doing it. It's society. The only difference is that cops infringe on our rights. It's much easier for the cops to do it on an everyday basis.

> K: Is it somehow different when the police infringe on your rights than when regular Joe citizen infringes on your rights?
>
> J: Yes it is definitely different. Oh my gosh, incredibly different! First off, the police are paid individuals to protect your rights. They are there to actually protect your rights. To help you in your case of need. Who are you supposed to turn to when the very people that are supposed to protect you then are infringing on them?

Jesse argues that police–minority relations are reflective of larger racialization and criminalization processes in the sociolegal realm. The infringement of rights by the state via racial profiling processes is a key concern in his narrative. The contrast with the state's role in theory and how it operates in practice in communities of color is evident in his comment about the protectors of rights in practice often violate rights. Ultimately, Jesse's connection of racial profiling processes to the larger social realm is at the crux of the current project—racial profiling is a manifestation of broader social, political, and legal realms that structure racial and ethnic experiences in the contemporary era.

CONCLUSION

The narratives in this chapter demonstrate the complexity of the vicarious experience in explaining "perceptions" of being racially profiled. I attempted to contextualize Foucault's panopticon effect—the awareness of constant surveillance and power dynamics by the state—experienced by many people of color into the realm of vicarious experience as discussed in the current literature on racial profiling. I also frame the break from citizenship that occurs with panopticonism processes of criminalization within DuBois's notion of double consciousness: Awareness of the panopticon, that is, awareness of surveillance and a lack of both physical and mental freedom, reflects an awareness of a denial to full citizenship protections from the state. I also engaged what Russell[22] and others refer to as "the lesson." The lesson is advice and admonitions passed down across generations among communities of color that offer wisdom on how to deal with a racial state. I argue that this theoretical approach—vicarious experience, panopticonism, double consciousness, and the lesson—is crucial to understanding why the racialized traffic stop is a much more socially divisive and harmful encounter than current literature on racial profiling suggests.

The panopticon theoretical framework provides the underlying rationale for both vicarious experience and the related issues of collective memory and the lesson. The racial state engages in hypersurveillance of communities of color and, in doing so, projects its capacity to dominate. These processes have a long racial history in America. Although eventual constitutional protections against state intervention and related repression were presented ideologically as "justice and liberty for all," the practice of equal treatment under the law has never been fully carried out for communities of color at large. As discussed by Feagin[23] and others, these processes of racial oppression are met with resistance. Resistance not only implies opposition to power dynamics but the development of coping strategies to withstand the everydayness of racial injustice. Hence, as evidenced in the preceding narratives, people of color develop a collective and complex understanding of the social world.

I argue that while these processes may be considered in the vicarious experience realm as discussed in the current racial profiling literature, these experiences are captured only perfunctorily in the current literature's treatment. When the current literature discusses the vicarious experience effect in perceptions of racial profiling, it generally only provides "information from family and friends . . . " in defining vicarious experience. This characterization of vicariousness, when combined with popular discourse that suggests people of color keep notions of racial oppression alive in the contemporary era in part because they continue to discuss historical racial events collectively, severely limits our understanding of the complexity of vicarious experiences. The critical analysis forwarded here positions these vicarious experiences as fundamental knowledge garnered by communities of color that are in turn circulated generationally as a means to negotiate the racial state.

NOTES

1. Bell, Derrick. 1992. *Faces at the Bottom of the Well: The Permanence of Racism*. New York: Basic Books, p. 198.
2. Weitzer, Ronald, and Steven A. Tuch. 2006. *Race and Policing in America: Conflict and Reform*. Cambridge, UK: Cambridge University Press, p. 19.
3. Bonilla-Silva, Eduardo. 2003. *Racism without Racists: Color-Blind Racism and the Persistence of Racial Inequality in the United States*. Lanham, MD: Rowman & Littlefield; see also Bonilla-Silva, Eduardo, and Gianpaolo Baiocchi. 2001. "Anything but Racism: How Sociologists Limit the Significance of Racism." *Race & Society* 4: 117–31.
4. Moore, Wendy Leo. 2007. *Reproducing Racism: White Space, Elite Law Schools, and Racial Inequality*. Lanham, MD: Rowman & Littlefield.
5. Zuberi, Tukufu, and Eduardo Bonilla-Silva. 2008. *White Logic, White Methods: Racism and Methodology*. Lanham, MD: Rowman & Littlefield.
6. Russell, Katheryn K. 1998. *The Color of Crime: Racial Hoaxes, White Fear, Black Protectionism, Police Harassment, and Other Macroaggressions*. New York: New York University Press.
7. Feagin, Joe R. 2006. *Systemic Racism: A Theory of Oppression*. New York: Routledge.
8. Barlow, David E., and Melissa Hickman Barlow. 2000. *Police in a Multicultural Society: An American Story*. Long Grove, IL: Waveland Press.
9. Foucault, Michel. 1977. *Discipline and Punish: The Birth of the Prison*. (Translated by Alan Sheridan). New York: Random House, p. 101.
10. Foucault, *Discipline and Punish*, p. 101.
11. Collins, Patricia Hill. 2000. *Black Feminist Thought: Knowledge, Consciousness, and the Politics of Empowerment*. New York: Routledge.
12. Blau, Judith R., and Eric S. Brown. 2001. "DuBois and Diasporic Identity: The *Veil* and the *Unveiling* Project." *Sociological Theory* 19: 219–33, p. 220.
13. Feagin, Joe R., and Melvin P. Sikes. 1994. *Living with Racism: The Black Middle-Class Experience*. Boston: Beacon Press.

14. Feagin, *Systemic Racism.*
15. Zuberi and Bonilla-Silva, *White Logic, White Methods.*
16. Feagin and Sikes, *Living with Racism.*
17. Feagin, *Systemic Racism.*
18. Collins, *Black Feminist Thought.*
19. Bonilla-Silva, *Racism without Racists.*
20. Foucault, *Discipline and Punish*, p. 187.
21. Pettit, Becky, and Bruce Western. 2004. "Mass Imprisonment and the Life Course: Race and Class Inequality in U.S. Incarceration." *American Sociological Review* 69: 151–69.
22. Russell, *The Color of Crime.*
23. Feagin, *Systemic Racism.*

Conclusion

I was raised to believe that white was true and lawful.

Richard Perez[1]

The above is a quote from a student of mine who manages to put into one brief sentence what I hope this book addresses. The quote itself is a reflection on how we come to know truth and knowledge. There are many in the field of criminology who are attune to the logic of white supremacy ideology and who have over the years made their own and collective efforts and calls to address the dominant paradigm of race in America. My desire is to add my voice and the voices of my respondents to one particular area of criminology, mainstream racial profiling studies. A deconstruction of mainstream research on racial profiling is to make the case that the hegemonic paradigm for examining this phenomenon is derived, partially at least, from a white logic/white methodology. I have attempted to demonstrate how this explains how members of society (via racialized knowledge circulating in academia, the political sphere, and the general public arena) have come to connect racial status with truth and lawfulness, or with fear and criminality, and how this manifests in the racially oppressive practice of profiling. I have attempted to show how traffic stops of people of color are not the bounded, troublesome encounter concerned with attitude projections toward individualized police officers or police officers in general, as reflected in the vast majority of racial profiling research to date. Instead, my examination demonstrates, through qualitative analysis and an engagement of critical race theory, that these traffic stops are reflective of much greater sociopolitical realms and are viewed as landmark, watershed moments that change one's relationship with the racial state through a break in citizenship. I have attempted to demonstrate how legal maneuvers in the post-Civil Rights era, embodied by the 1996 *Whren v. United States* decision on the constitutionality of the pretextual traffic stop, are mere continuations of racialized law and law enforcement practices that date back to the slave codes.

Like the sage who reminds us of important things when we most need to hear, lately I am reminded that I may fail in my efforts or I may succeed, and either way will not be the first or last time that happens. I look at the students in my criminology classes, a diverse group, relatively, at the California State University in Southern California. Many are the students who want to be law enforcement agents and while I discourage them from having expectations of a cop-shop framework in my critical criminology-oriented classroom, I know that those who stay, resistant perhaps to the very end, benefit on some level from the course that is decidedly not in the cop-shop framework. It is to the students like Richard, however, that I feel most bound to when I call out the discipline of criminology on its white logic orientations with racial profiling research. If Richard has aspirations toward law in some way, shape, or form, and is only exposed to the hegemonic paradigm of white logic in the academy, he will indeed come away with the sense that "white is true and lawful." One likely reason is the way people of color are represented as on the other side of law, standing next to crime, the main characters on the American criminological stage. With the Obama presidency, one question to ask is, will having a person of color in such a powerful position influence racial representations in the white mind? Will the practices of the racial state and affiliated social institutions change?

Because of the social reproduction of racial inequality in our educational system, very few whites are familiar with the racial realities of the George Washingtons and Thomas Jeffersons in their founding of this country. Through my exposure to great and brave scholars (from whom I have learned that I must put myself in the fire if I am to genuinely reflect their teachings!), I have been educated about the racial attitudes, behaviors, and policies of the "founding fathers," including those who are attributed with creating our most sacred of all legal documents, the United States Constitution. I know when the Constitution talks of liberty and justice for all, it did not mean for *all people* but rather for a very particular segment of society that the founding fathers themselves reflected. As stated by Mills,[2] "We the People" meant "We the (white) People," and indeed further, it meant *we the white male elites*. The Constitution serves as the ultimate discursive tool to organize the legal means of white supremacy ideology. Yet until Joe Feagin's dream of a new Constitutional Convention comes to fruition, we hold up (ideally, if not in practice) the

Constitution they created. Thus, when I have students in my classes or, as I anticipate, readers of this work, suggesting I am anti-law enforcement, I will remind them that one can't have it both ways. Either the Constitution is the discursive, white supremacy ideology cornerstone as I describe it above or it is something to abide by at face value—that there are equal protections under the law and liberty and justice for all. If you accept the former, then one of the giant pillars of white supremacy ideology falls and hits you squarely on the head, a (blessed) injury you will never "recover" from. If you accept the latter, then the data and analysis presented in this book should be viewed as a defense of the Constitution, that the author is indeed a *defender* of the Constitution (in its color-blind text) and not anti-law enforcement! One can't have it both ways.

Or can one? In the era of color-blind racism,[3] the strange enigma to be explained is how can so many white Americans proclaim they are not racist and that racism does not matter that much anymore while all markers of social well-being continue to be racially ordered? To apply this to racial profiling research, how is it that mainstream criminology can have at the top of their research agenda for years the phenomenon of racialized law enforcement and, at least initially, with each passing year make improvements in how the phenomenon is measured, with each passing year and increasingly sophisticated methods demonstrating a strong "correlation" between racial minority status and likelihood of being stopped by the police, then turn to "perceptions" of what makes folks of color believe law enforcement is targeting them? How is it that the decade-long focus by mainstream criminology on racial profiling has yet in any serious way examined the phenomenon as one of racial oppression, given the fundamental use of race in the United States to determine law and law enforcement since the arrival of the first slave ship in colonial America in 1619, during the Black Codes following abolition, and through the Jim Crow era of legal segregation that officially "ended" in MY lifetime yet believe that these now-institutionalized legal practices can be effectively struck down by decree and not substantively remain entrenched in state practices? How is it that mainstream criminology racial profiling research can time and again acknowledge the critical methodological importance of *the voice* in examinations of racialized law enforcement yet neglect to conduct in-depth interviews with those folks who are central actors in the phenomenon—primarily young men of color—to explore what the experience of racialized law enforcement means to them?

I argued in this book that all of the concerns described above are a function of the white logic tendency in mainstream criminology. The disciplines of sociology and criminology, as with other purveyors of knowledge, are a major influence on what the general public, the academy, and public policy administrators focus on. That is the import of the long history of calls to examine the production of knowledge as it is manufactured, disseminated, and engaged in the racial state that is the United States.

I end with a particularly moving moment from the film *The Color of Fear*.[4] A documentary about racism, it centers on a small focus group of Asian, black, Latino, and white men. The filmmaker, Lee, and other members of the group exert a great deal of energy (both in subtle and assertive expressions) trying to get the dominant white male, David, to recognize that their stories of racial oppression are valid. With all men mentally, physically, and spiritually exhausted at this point, Lee tries once more—"David," he says, "what if it *is* true? What if it *is* true what we say?" The camera, now on David, captures a look in his eye that is all at once self-recognition, rejection, urgency, and awareness that he can't go back. It was a struggle, to be sure, but on some level, David got it. What if it *is* true what we say? What if it *is* true?

NOTES

1. 2008. Personal communication.
2. Mills, Charles W. 1997. *The Racial Contract*. Ithaca, NY: Cornell University Press.
3. Bonilla-Silva, Eduardo. 2003. *Racism without Racists: Color-Blind Racism and the Persistence of Racial Inequality in the United States*. Lanham, MD: Rowman & Littlefield.
4. Lee Mun Wah. 1994. *The Color of Fear*. Oakland, CA: Stir-Fry Productions. Videorecording.

Appendix A

Methodology

I am guided by Bonilla-Silva's[1] work suggesting the operation of race in society reproduces racial inequality because it is "embedded in normal operations of social institutions," and Feagin's[2] argument regarding the *everyday* quality of racism that reflects larger racist forces in society. These two orientations are appropriate as the regularity of racial profiling processes in society emerges from normalized and racialized practices of the state that manifest in the traffic stop.

My choice of method—the in-depth interview—is important because we know little about the experiences of social actors who have experienced racial profiling. During 2005–2006, I collected interview data from twenty-six individuals. The race/ethnic/gender status of my respondents includes ten Latinos, two Latinas, five black males, six black females, one biracial female, and two white males. The first of the two primary locations for data collection is a South Texas city with a population of approximately 280,000 (U.S. Census Bureau). Demographically, the city is 2 percent Asian, 5 percent African American, 54 percent Latino (primarily Mexican American), and 74 percent white. The second location is a Southeast Texas region with a population of approximately 140,000 (U.S. Census Bureau). Demographically, the region is 5 percent Asian, 13 percent African American, 19 percent Latino, and 74 percent white. Because of its substantial Latino population, the South Texas locale provides access to a relatively underresearched group in the police–minority relations literature. The second location was primarily chosen out of convenience. Research participants were recruited through networks I have in both areas, and then snowball sampling was used to recruit other research participants. These networks included contacts in university settings, religious institutions, the criminal justice realm, and the community at large. Potential respondents were informed that the general nature of the research concerned their experiences with law enforcement where they believed racial or ethnic status factored into the encounter. Research participants were assured of anonymity. While the sample is nonrandom, efforts were made to include a sample in which the "language, understandings, and orientations" of the sample is reflective of the larger experiences of communities of color.[3]

The current study quotes heavily from these interviews, with an emphasis on respondents who presented detailed and illustrative articulations of their experiences with racial profiling. Though not all respondents are directly quoted in the current study due to the directed topic of examination, their insight was useful in the organization and theorizing on the project. The interviews, conducted, audiotaped, and transcribed by me, lasted between thirty minutes to more than two hours. I felt it was necessary that I handle transcriptions in order to refresh and expand on my initial reflections of particularly important points of the interview. I did not engage in traditional conversation analysis, such as accounting for pauses, incoherence, and other speech details, in large part due to the evident flow of the interviews. To put this in context, an earlier research project of mine involved in-depth interviews with primarily white police officers about police–minority relations and racial profiling specifically.[4] The data collected did call for special attention to pauses and incoherence in speech, for example, as these and other indicators of tension in the interview were immediately evident. Conversely, the interviews with people of color about their racial profiling experiences did not include similar discursive stumbling and incoherence evident in the police interviews. Indeed, the current respondents were quite direct and genuinely expressive in their accounts.

All respondents were assigned a pseudonym. While a data sheet was used to collect anonymous demographic information, a pretested, semistructured interview schedule was used that consisted of a series of open-ended questions to facilitate a conversational style interview format (see Appendix B for general questions). Generally, respondents were first asked to give their definitions and impressions of racial profiling, after which I generally inquired as to whether they had a specific instance they could relay where they believed racial or ethnic status played a role in an encounter they had with law enforcement. Respondents were not subjected to a strict format but encouraged to discuss issues surrounding the general topic.

Following Rockquemore's approach to analyzing interview data, I first devoted time to distilling relevant topic data from nonrelevant information before focusing on emergent themes and similarities present in the data.[5] Each interview was listened to more than once and the resulting transcripts were read, in some cases, numerous times. I then collapsed the subthemes that emerged into more general categories. For example, the general theme of citizenship discussed in chapter 5 was created after the emergence of common references to accountability, knowledge of rights discourses, or direct claims to constitutional protections as indicated by one respondent's statement that "You belong in our society if you are treated by the Constitution and the Bill of Rights. That's when you belong."

Ultimately, after fine-tuning my research agenda to address the specific issue of the "perception"-based studies in the current racial profiling literature and its focus on personal and vicarious experiences with law enforcement, I sorted the narratives as they fit into these two general categories. I then contextualized the data as it applied to the themes of citizenship, resistance, panopticonism, and "the lesson."

The limitations of the current study include its inability to contextualize findings within a similar, specifically qualitative, literature because of the lack of scholarship currently available. Some readers may find the number of respondents to be small. However, while a more sizable sample would permit me to do more comparative analysis, for example, the heart of qualitative work is not determined by quantity. I was asked why I wouldn't want to quantify the breakdown of respondents who responded similarly to a particular theme. As a qualitative researcher, the *theme* is the important part of the research. I could very well accommodate the suggestion yet understand the quantification—*x* percent of the respondents agreed—has less priority when the purpose of the research is to understand the meaning and experience of the racialized traffic stop on citizens of color. With the current study, not all people of color need experience limited citizenship through racial profiling processes and not all whites need be granted the "ideal" of citizenship to make the current study an important contribution to our knowledge of the operation of racial and ethnic status in society, and more specifically, as it affects the criminal justice system. Another critic referred to my data as *anecdotal*, a term often used to denigrate qualitative work. Critical scholarship views the meanings and understandings that emerge from the narrative realm as possessing intrinsic value.

NOTES

1. Bonilla-Silva, Eduardo. 1997. "Rethinking Racism: Toward a Structural Interpretation." *American Sociological Review* 62: 465–80.

2. Feagin, Joe R. 2006. *Systemic Racism: A Theory of Oppression*. New York: Routledge.

3. Bolton, Jr., Kenneth, and Joe R. Feagin. 2004. *Black in Blue: African-American Police Officers and Racism*. New York: Routledge, p. 39.

4. Glover, Karen S. 2007. "Police Discourse on Racial Profiling." *Journal of Contemporary Criminal Justice* 23: 239–47.

5. Rockquemore, Kerry Ann. 2002. "Negotiating the Color Line: The Gendered Process of Racial Identity Construction among Black/White Biracial Women." *Gender and Society* 16: 485–503.

Appendix B

Interview Schedule

Have you heard the term racial profiling?
What does that mean to you?
When you think about mistreatment by the police, what kinds of things come up?
Have you ever experienced any mistreatment by the police?
If so, what happened? (ask about what they were doing, interactions with police, demographics of officer, insulting language, force or threat of force, ticketed/searched, attitude, spatial issues, type of car, etc.)
Do you think you've ever been racially profiled or mistreated by the police?
If so, what happened? (ask about what they were doing, interactions with police, demographics of officer, insulting language, force or threat of force, ticketed/searched, attitude, spatial issues, type of car, etc.)
What makes you think race was involved?
Why did the officer say they were stopping you?
What did you think about this?
Some people say that it makes sense that the police pay more attention to blacks and Latinos because they make up the majority of people in prison. What do you think of this argument or way of thinking?
What about the majority of blacks and Latinos who are not involved in any crime. Are they affected by racial profiling?
Do you think racial profiling happens often?
What makes you think so?

What kinds of things do you think about after you've had an experience with the police?
How do you feel?
How do you cope with these feelings?
How do you think this kind of experience influences your attitudes toward the police in general?
Research shows that blacks and Latinos are more disapproving of the police than whites. Why do you think this is so?
Now if we could talk a little about how you feel the police treat people in general. Do you think blacks or Latinos in your neighborhood are treated fairly by the police compared to how whites are treated? Please give me an example if you can.
Why do you think that happens?
Has anyone you know—friends or family—been racially profiled or mistreated by the police?
What happened?
How did you find out about it?
Do you and your friends and family ever talk about how the police treat you?
What kinds of things do you talk about?
Do you discuss how to "act" around the police?
If so, what types of things do you do differently?
Now we're going to talk a little about the neighborhood that you live in now. How do you describe the neighborhood?
Do you feel pretty safe here during the day?
How about at night—do you feel safe?
Do you feel like the police in your neighborhood take care of things?
Can you give me an example?
What about other areas of town that you go to?
Are there any areas of town where you feel like the police act differently to you than they do in your neighborhood?
If so, how do they act?
How does it make you feel?
How do you feel about the police in those places?
Do you feel like you trust the police in your neighborhood?
What does trust mean to you?
What about the police in general?
Say there was a problem with the police in your neighborhood. Do you feel like you could do something about the problem?
Why?
The next thing we could talk about is the media. There are a lot of TV shows about the police, the courts, etc. What do you think about these shows?

Some people say these shows pretty much show how things are with the police but others say these shows exaggerate things between the police and the people they deal with. What do you think?

Some people say TV and newspapers have a lot to do with how much we like the police. What do you think?

Have you ever wondered how the police make decisions about who to stop, say if there are a bunch of people speeding down the highway?

What do you think the police base most of their decisions on in these cases? (neutrality, objectivity, consistency)

Some people, when they're asked about whether they think the police have stopped them because they are black or Latino, say sometimes it depends on whether the officer showed enough respect and fairness during the stop. What do you think about this?

In your experience, how does an officer show respect and fairness? Please give me an example if you can.

Finally, I was wondering what you think of this research that I'm doing and if you have any comments or questions to ask me.

Bibliography

Armour, Jody David. 1997. *Negrophobia and reasonable racism: The hidden costs of being black in America*. New York: New York University Press.

Barak, Gregg, Jeanne Flavin, and Paul Leighton. 2007. *Class, race, gender, and crime: The social realities of justice in America*. Lanham, MD: Rowman & Littlefield.

Barlow, David E., and Melissa Hickman Barlow. 2000. *Police in a multicultural society: An American story*. Long Grove, IL: Waveland Press.

Becker, Gary S. 1993. "Nobel lecture: The economic way of looking at behavior." *Journal of Political Economy* 101:385–409.

Bell, Derrick. 1992. *Faces at the bottom of the well: The permanence of racism*. New York: Basic Books.

———. 2000. *Race, racism, and American law*. New York: Aspen Publishers.

Bennett, Gary G., Marcellus M. Merritt, Christopher L. Edwards, and John J. Sollers III. 2004. Perceived racism and affective responses to ambiguous interpersonal interactions among African American men. *American Behavioral Scientist* 47:963–76.

Bennett, William J., John J. Diilulio, and John P. Walters. 1996. *Body count: Moral poverty . . . and how to win America's war against crime and drugs*. New York: Simon & Schuster.

Berry, Mary Frances. 1994. *Black resistance, white law: A history of constitutional racism in America*. New York: Penguin Press.

Blau, Judith R., and Eric S. Brown. 2001. DuBois and diasporic identity: The *veil* and the *unveiling* project. *Sociological Theory* 19:219–33.

Bolton, Jr., Kenneth, and Joe R. Feagin. 2004. *Black in blue: African-American police officers and racism*. New York: Routledge.

Bonilla-Silva, Eduardo. 1997. Rethinking racism: Toward a structural interpretation. *American Sociological Review* 62:465–80.

———. 2003. *Racism without racists: Color-blind racism and the persistence of racial inequality in the United States*. Lanham, MD: Rowman & Littlefield.

Bonilla-Silva, Eduardo, and Gianpaolo Baiocchi. 2001. Anything but racism: How sociologists limit the significance of racism. *Race & Society* 4:117-31.

Brown, Ben, and William Reed Benedict. 2002. Perceptions of the police: Past findings, methodological issues, conceptual issues, and policy implications. *Policing: An International Journal of Police Strategies & Management* 25:543–80.

Brown, Michael K., Martin Carnoy, Elliot Currie, Troy Duster, David B. Oppenheimer, Marjorie M. Schultz, and David Wellman. 2003. *White-washing race: The myth of a color-blind society*. Berkeley: University of California Press, ix.

Brunson, Rod K. 2007. "Police don't like black people": African-American young men's accumulated police experiences. *Criminology & Public Policy* 6:71–101.

Buerger, Michael E., and Amy Farrell. 2002. The evidence of racial profiling: differing Interpretations of documented and unofficial sources. *Police Quarterly* 5:272–305.

Burawoy, Michael. 1991. The extended case method. Pp. 271–87 in *Ethnography unbound: Power and resistance in the modern metropolis,* Michael Burawoy, Alice Burton, Ann Arnett Ferguson, and Kathryn J. Fox, editors. Berkeley: University of California Press.

Collins, Patricia Hill. 2000. *Black feminist thought: Knowledge, consciousness, and the politics of empowerment*. New York: Routledge.

Cook, Dee. 1999. Racism, citizenship and exclusion. Pp. 136–57 in *Racism & criminology*, Dee Cook and Barbara Hudson, editors. London: Sage Publications.

Cooper, Christopher. 2003. Unlawful motives and race-based arrest for minor offenses. *Justice Policy Journal* 1:3–17.

Covington, Jeannette. 1995. Racial classification in criminology: The reproduction of racialized crime. In *Sociological Forum Special Issue: African Americans and Sociology: A Critical Analysis* 10:547–68.

———. 2001. Round up the usual suspects: Racial profiling and the war on drugs. Pp. 27–42 in *Petit apartheid in the U.S. criminal justice system: The dark figure of racism*, Dragan Milovanovic and Katheryn K. Russell, editors. Durham, NC: Carolina Academic Press.

Crawford, Kimberly A. 1995. Pretext seizures. *FBI Law Enforcement Bulletin* 64:28–33, p. 28.

Crenshaw, Kimberlé, Neil Gotanda, Gary Peller, and Kendall Thomas. 1995. *Critical race theory: The key writings that informed the movement*. New York: New Press.

Davis, Angela Y. 1983. *Women, race, and class*. New York: Vintage Books.

Davis, Angela J. 1997. Race, cops, and traffic stops. *University of Miami Law Review* 51:6.

Davis, Peggy C. 2000 [1989]. Law as microaggression. Pp. 141–51 in *Critical Race Theory: The Cutting Edge*, Richard Delgado and Jean Stefancic, editors. Philadelphia, PA: Temple University Press, 149.

Delgado, Richard. 1999. Citizenship. Pp. 247–52 in *Race, identity, and citizenship: A reader*, Rodolfo D. Torres, Louis F. Miron, and Jonathan Xavier Inda, editors. Malden, MA: Blackwell Publishers.

Delgado, Rodrigo, and Jean Stefancic, eds. 2000. *Critical race theory: The cutting edge*. Philadelphia, PA: Temple University Press.

DuBois, W. E. B. 1986. *Writings: The suppression of the slave trade; The souls of black folks; Dusk of dawn; Essays and articles*. New York: Literary Classics of the United States-Library of America.

Dunham, Roger G., Geoffrey P. Alpert, Meghan S. Stroshine, and Katherine Bennett. 2005. Transforming citizens into suspects: Factors that influence the formation of police suspicion. *Police Quarterly* 8:366–93.

Dvale, Steiner. 1996. *An introduction to qualitative research interviewing*. Thousand Oaks, CA: Sage Publications.

Engel, Robin Shepard. 2005. Citizens' perceptions of distributive and procedural injustice during traffic stops with police. *Journal of Research in Crime and Delinquency* 42:445–81.

Engel, Robin Shepard, Jennifer M. Calnon, and Thomas J. Bernard. 2002. Theory and racial profiling: Shortcomings and future directions in research. *Justice Quarterly* 19:249–73.

Esposito, Luigi, and John W. Murphy. 1999. Desensitizing Herbert Blumer's work on race relations: Recent applications of his group position theory to the study of contemporary racial prejudice. *Sociological Quarterly* 40:397–410.

Feagin, Joe R. 2001. *Racist America: Roots, current realities, and future reparations*. New York: Routledge.

———. 2006. *Systemic racism: A theory of oppression*. New York: Routledge.

Feagin, Joe R., and Melvin P. Sikes. 1994. *Living with racism: The black middle-class experience*. Boston: Beacon Press.

Feingold, Russ. 2004. Feingold introduces the End Racial Profiling Act of 2004. February 26, 2004 press release. Retrieved December 14, 2004 from http://feingold.senate.gov/releases/04/02/2004304407.html.

Fine, Michelle. 2006. Bearing witness: Methods for researching repression and resistance—A textbook for critical research. *Social Justice Research* 19:83–108.

Fireside, Harvey. 2004. *Separate and unequal: Homer Plessy and the Supreme Court decision that legalized racism*. New York: Carroll & Graf Publishers.

Foucault, Michel. 1977. *Discipline and punish: The birth of the prison*. (Translated by Alan Sheridan). New York: Random House.

Frankenberg, Ruth. 1994. *White women, race matters: The social construction of whiteness*. New York: Routledge.

Gabbidon, Shaun L., Helen Taylor Greene, and Vernetta D. Young, eds. 2002. *African American classics in criminology & criminal justice*. Thousand Oaks, CA: Sage Publications.

Glover, Karen S. 2007. Police discourse on racial profiling. *Journal of Contemporary Criminal Justice* 23:239–47.

Gross, Ariela. 2008. History, race, and prediction: Comments on Harcourt's *Against Prediction*. *Law and School Inquiry* 33:233–42.

Gross, Samuel R., and Debra Livingston. 2002. Racial profiling under attack. *Columbia Law Review* 102:1413.

Haenfler, Ross. 2004. Rethinking subcultural resistance: Core values of the straight edge movement. *Journal of Contemporary Ethnography* 33:406–36.

Hagan, John, and Celesta Albonetti. 1982. Race, class, and the perception of criminal injustice in America. *American Journal of Sociology* 88:329–55.

Hall, Christopher. 1998. Challenging selective enforcement of traffic regulations after the disharmonic convergence: *Whren v. United States, United States v. Armstrong*, and the evolution of police discretion. *Texas Law Review* 76:1083–123. 1108.

Hall, John C. 1996. Pretext Traffic Stops: *Whren v. United States*. Retrieved December 6, 2004, p. 5, from www.fbi.gov/publications/leb/1996/nov965.txt.

Haney Lopez, Ian F. 1996. *White by law: The legal construction of race*. New York: New York University Press.

Harcourt, Bernard E. 2001. *Illusion of order: The false promise of broken windows policing*. Cambridge, MA: Harvard University Press.

———. 2007. *Against prediction: Profiling, policing, and punishing in an actuarial age*. Chicago: University of Chicago Press.

Harris, David A. 1997. "Driving while black" and all other traffic offenses: The Supreme Court and pretextual traffic stops. *Journal of Criminal Law and Criminology* 87:544–82, p. 549.

———. 2002. *Profiles in injustice: Why racial profiling cannot work*. New York: New Press.

Jamal, Samina. 2005. Critical ethnography. Pp. 225–40 in *Critical issues in anti-racist research methodologies,* George J. Sefa Dei and Gurpreet Singh Johal, editors. New York: Peter Lang Publishing.

Johnson, Sheri Lynn. 2001. Racial derogation in prosecutor's closing arguments. Pp. 79–102 in *Petit apartheid in the U.S. criminal justice system: The dark figure of racism,* Dragan Milovanovic and Katheryn K. Russell, editors. Durham, NC: Carolina Academic Press.

Jones, Kathleen B. 1990. Citizenship in a woman-friendly polity. *Signs* 15:781–812.

Katz, Michael B., and Thomas J. Sugrue, eds. 1998. *W.E.B. DuBois, race, and the city: The Philadelphia Negro and its legacy*. Philadelphia: University of Pennsylvania Press.

Kennelly, Ivy. 1999. "That single-mother element": How white employers typify black women. *Gender and Society* 13:168–92.

Kerber, Linda K. 1998. *No constitutional right to be ladies: Women and the obligations of citizenship*. New York: Hill and Wang.

King, Joyce E. 1997. Dysconscious racism: Ideology, identity, and miseducation. Pp. 128–34 in *Critical white studies: Looking behind the mirror,* Richard Delgado and Jean Stefancic, editors. Philadelphia, PA: Temple University Press.

Klockars, Carl B. 1974. *The professional fence*. New York: Free Press.

Lamberth, John. 1998. *Driving while black: A statistician proves that prejudice still rules the road*. Retrieved September 3, 2002 from www.hartford-hwp.com/archives/45a/192.html.

Lanier, Mark M., and Stuart Henry. 2004. *Essential criminology*. Boulder, CO: Westview Press.

Lynch, Michael J. 1996. Class, race, gender and criminology: Structured choices and the life course. Pp. 3–38 in *Race, gender, and class in criminology: The intersection,* Martin D. Schwartz and Dragan Milovanovic, editors. New York: Garland.

Lynch, Michael J., Danielle McGurrin, and Melissa Fenwick. 2004. Disappearing act: The representation of corporate crime research in criminological literature. *Journal of Criminal Justice* 32:389–98.

MacDonald, Heather. 2003. *Are cops racist?* Chicago: Ivan R. Dee.

Marchetti, Elena. 2008. Intersectional race and gender analyses: Why legal processes just don't get it. *Social Legal Studies* 1:155–74.

Marshall, Anna-Maria, and Scott Barclay. 2003. In their own words: How ordinary people construct the legal world. *Law and Social Inquiry* 28:617–28.

Marshall, Thomas Humphrey. 1964. *Class, citizenship, and social development: Essays*. Garden City, NY: Doubleday.

Martinez, Ramiro. 2007. Incorporating Latinos and immigrants into policing research. *Criminology & Public Policy* 6:57–64.

McLaughlin, T. 1992. Citizenship, diversity and education: A philosophical perspective. *Journal of Moral Education* 21:235–51.

Meeks, Kenneth. 2000. *Driving while black: Highways, shopping malls, taxicabs, sidewalks: How to fight back if you are a victim of racial profiling*. New York: Broadway Books.

Milazzo, Carl, and Ron Hansen. 1999 (Nov.). "Race relations in police operations: A legal and ethical perspective." Paper presented at the 106th annual conference of the International Association of Chiefs of Police, Charlotte, NC.

Mills, Charles W. 1997. *The racial contract*. Ithaca, NY: Cornell University Press.

Moore, Wendy Leo. 2007. *Reproducing racism: White space, elite law schools, and racial inequality*. Lanham, MD: Rowman & Littlefield.

Nielson, Laura Beth. 2000. Situating legal consciousness: Experiences and attitudes of ordinary citizens about law and street harassment. *Law & Society Review* 34:1055–90.

Omi, Michael, and Howard Winant. 1994. *Racial formation in the United States from the 1960s to the 1990s*. New York: Routledge.

Parker, Karen F., John M. MacDonald, Geoffrey P. Alpert, Michael R. Smith, and Alex R. Piquero. 2004. A contextual study of racial profiling: Assessing the theoretical rationale for the study of racial profiling at the local level. *American Behavioral Scientist* 47:943–62.

Parker, Keith D., Anne B. Onyekwuluje, and Komanduri S. Murty. 1995. African-Americans' attitudes toward the police: A multivariate study. *Journal of Black Studies* 25:396–409.

Parker, Laurence, and Marvin Lynn. 2002. What's race got to do with it? Critical race theory's conflicts with and connections to qualititative research, methodology and epistomology. *Qualitative Inquiry* 8:7–22.

Pate, Antony M., and Lorie A. Fridell. 1993. *Police use of force: Official reports, citizen complaints, and legal consequences*. Washington, DC: Police Foundation.

Petrocelli, Matthew, Alex R. Piquero, and Michael R. Smith. 2003. Conflict theory and racial profiling: An empirical analysis of police traffic stop data. *Journal of Criminal Justice* 31:1–11.

Pettit, Becky, and Bruce Western. 2004. Mass imprisonment and the life course: Race and class inequality in U.S. incarceration. *American Sociological Review* 69:151–69.

Phillips, Anne. 1993. *Democracy and difference*. University Park: Pennsylvania State University Press.

Piquero, Alex R., Zenta Gomez-Smith, and Lynn Langton. 2004. Discerning unfairness where others may not: Low self-control and unfair sanction perceptions. *Criminology* 42:699–733.

Ramirez, Deborah, Jack McDevitt, and Amy Farrell. 2000. A resource guide on racial profiling data collection systems: Promising practices and lessons learned. Monograph. Washington, DC: U.S. Department of Justice.

Reitzel, John D., and Alex R. Piquero. 2006. Does it exist? Studying citizens' attitudes of racial profiling. *Police Quarterly* 9:161–83.

Reitzel, John D., Stephen K. Rice, and Alex R. Piquero. 2004. Lines and shadows: Perceptions of racial profiling and the Hispanic experience. *Journal of Criminal Justice* 32:607–16.

Rockquemore, Kerry Ann. 2002. Negotiating the color line: The gendered process of racial identity construction among black/white biracial women. *Gender and Society* 16:485–503.

Rosaldo, Renato. 1999. Cultural citizenship, inequality, and multiculturalism. Pp. 253–61 in *Race, identity, and citizenship: A reader,* Rodolfo D. Torres, Louis F. Miron, and Jonathan Xavier Inda, editors. Malden, MA: Blackwell Publishers.

Russell, Katheryn K. 1998. *The color of crime: Racial hoaxes, white fear, black protectionism, police harassment, and other macroaggressions*. New York: New York University Press.

———. 2001a. Racial profiling: A status report of the legal, legislative, and empirical literature. *Rutgers Race & The Law Review* 3:61.

———. 2001b. Development of a black criminology and the role of the black criminologist. Pp. 279–92 in *African American Classics in Criminology & Criminal Justice,* Shaun L. Gabbidon, Helen Taylor Greene, and Vernetta D. Young, editors. Thousand Oaks, CA: Sage Publications.

Russell, Margaret M. 1992. Entering great America: Reflections on race and the convergence of progressive legal theory and practice. *Hastings Law Journal* 43:749–67.

Sampson, Robert J., and Dawn Jeglum Bartusch. 1998. Legal cynicism and (subcultural) tolerance of deviance: The neighborhood context of racial differences. *Law & Society Review* 32:777–804.

Shaw, Clifford. 1966. *The Jack-Roller: A delinquent boy's own Story*. Chicago: University of Chicago Press.

Shaw, Clifford R., and Henry D. McKay. 1942. *Juvenile delinquency and urban areas: A study of rates of delinquents in relation to differential characteristics of local communities in American cities*. Chicago: University of Chicago Press.

Sikes, Melvin P. 1975. *The administration of injustice*. New York: Harper & Row.

Solorzano, Daniel G., and Tara J. Yosso. 2002. Critical race methodology: Counter-storytelling as an analytical framework for education research. *Qualitative Inquiry* 8:23–44.

Strauss, Anselm, and Juliet Corbin. 1998. *Basics of qualitative research: Techniques and procedures for developing grounded theory*. Thousand Oaks, CA: Sage Publications.

Tierney, William G., and Yvonna S. Lincoln, eds. 1997. *Representation and the text: Re-framing the narrative voice*. Albany: State University of New York Press.

Tomaskovic-Devey, Donald, Marcinda Mason, and Matthew Zingraff. 2004. Looking for the driving while black phenomenon: Conceptualizing racial bias processes and their associated distributions. *Police Quarterly* 7:3–29.

Torres, Eden. 2003. *Chicana without apology: The new Chicana cultural studies*. New York: Routledge.

Tuch, Steven A., and Ronald Weitzer. 1997. The polls-trends: Racial differences in attitudes toward the police. *Public Opinion Quarterly* 61:642–63.

Twine, France Winddance, and Jonathan W. Warren. 2000. *Racing research, researching race: Methodological dilemmas in critical race studies*. New York: New York University Press.

Tyler, Tom, and Cheryl J. Wakslak. 2004. Profiling and police legitimacy: Procedural justice, attributions of motive, and acceptance of police authority. *Criminology* 42:253–82.

United Nations Committee on the Elimination of Racial Discrimination. 2001 (Aug. 6, Geneva). Reply from U.S. Assistant Attorney General Ralph F. Boyd, Jr., and U.S. Assistant Secretary of State Lorne Craner. Retrieved December 6, 2004, p. 3, from www.usdoj.gov/crt/speeches/boydgenevaqanda.htm.

U.S. Census Bureau. 2000. Retrieved January 2006 from www.census.gov.

van den Hoonaard, Will C. 1997. *Working with sensitizing concepts: Analytical field research*. Thousand Oaks, CA: Sage Publications.

vicarious. (n.d.). *Dictionary.com Unabridged (v 1.1)*. Retrieved March 03, 2007, from Dictionary.com website: Hhttp://dictionary.reference.com/browse/vicarious

Volpp, Leti. 2002. Critical race studies: The citizen and the terrorist. *UCLA Law Review* 49:575.

Lee Mun Wah. 1994. *The Color of Fear*. Oakland, CA: Stir-Fry Production

Wahab, Amar. 2005. Consuming narratives: Questioning authority and the politics of representation in social science research. Pp. 29–51 in *Critical issues in anti-racist research methodologies*, George J. Sefa Dei and Gurpreet Singh Johal, editors. New York: Peter Lang Publishing.

Walker, David. 2000. *David Walker's appeal to the coloured citizens of the world*, Peter P. Hinks, editor. University Park: Pennsylvania State University.

Ward, James D. 2002. Race, ethnicity, and law enforcement profiling: Implications for public policy. *Public Administration Review* 62:726–35.

Weitzer, Ronald. 2000. Racialized policing: Residents' perceptions in three neighborhoods. *Law & Society Review* 34:129–55.

Weitzer, Ronald, and Steven A. Tuch. 1999. Race, class, and perceptions of discrimination by the police. *Crime & Delinquency* 45:494–507.

———. 2002. Perceptions of racial profiling: Race, class, and personal experience. *Criminology* 40:435–56.

———. 2004. Race and perceptions of police misconduct. *Social Problems* 51:305–25.

———. 2005. Racially biased policing: Determinants of citizen perceptions. *Social Forces* 83:1009–30.

———. 2006. *Race and policing in America: Conflict and reform*. Cambridge, UK: Cambridge University Press.

West, Candace, and Sarah Fenstermaker. 1995. Doing difference. *Gender & Society* 9:8–37.

Western, Bruce. 2006. *Punishment and inequality in America.* New York: Russell Sage Foundation.

Whren v. United States. 1996. No. 95-5841. Supreme Court of the United States. Retrieved December 14, 2004 from http://web.lexis-nexis.com/universe/printdoc.

Williams, Patricia J. 1991. *The alchemy of race and rights.* Cambridge, MA: Harvard University Press.

Wilson, Bianca Della Marie, and Robin Lin Miller. 2002. Strategies for managing heterosexism used among African American gay and bisexual men. *Journal of Black Psychology* 28:371–91.

Wilson, George, Roger Dunham, and Geoffrey Alpert. 2004. Prejudice in police profiling: Assessing an overlooked aspect in prior research. *American Behavioral Scientist* 47:896–909.

Wilson, William Julius. 1978. *The declining significance of race: Blacks and changing American institutions.* Chicago: University of Chicago Press.

Withrow, Brian L. 2006. *Racial profiling: From rhetoric to reason.* Upper Saddle River, NJ: Pearson-Prentice Hall.

Wortley, Scott, John Hagan, and Ross Macmillan. 1997. Just des(s)erts? The racial polarization of perceptions of criminal injustice. *Law & Society Review* 31:637–76.

Yosso, Tara J., and David G. Garcia. 2007. "This is no slum!": A critical race theory analysis of community cultural wealth in Culture Clash's Chavez Ravine. *Aztlan: A Journal of Chicano Studies* 32:145–79.

Young, Alford. 2008. White ethnographers on the experiences of African American men: Then and now. Pp. 179–200 in *White logic, white methods: Racism and methodology,* Tukufu Zuberi and Eduardo Bonilla-Silva, editors. Lanham, MD: Rowman & Littlefield, p. 187.

Young, Iris Marion. 1989. Polity and group difference: A critique of the ideal of universal citizenship. *Ethics* 99:250–74.

Young, Vernetta D., and Helen Taylor Greene. 2000. Pedagogical reconstruction: Incorporating African American perspectives into the curriculum. Pp. 3–18 in *African American classics in criminology & criminal justice,* Shaun L. Gabbidon, Helen Taylor Greene, and Vernetta D. Young, editors. Thousand Oaks, CA: Sage Publications.

Zuberi, Tukufu. 2001. *Thicker than blood: How racial statistics lie.* Minneapolis: University of Minnesota Press.

Zuberi, Tukufu, and Eduardo Bonilla-Silva. 2008. *White logic, white methods: Racism and methodology.* Lanham, MD: Rowman & Littlefield.

Index

About the Author

Karen S. Glover is assistant professor of sociology in the Criminology and Justice Studies program at California State University San Marcos. She received her PhD in sociology from Texas A&M University. Her work focuses on racism in the law and in law enforcement.